How to Draw

Animals, Magical Creatures, aquatic creatures & objects

For Kids

Let's learn how to draw

Using the grid copy method makes drawing easier, this method is an amazing way to develop your drawing skills by working on observation of details.

The first thing to do : Grab a <u>pencil</u> and an <u>eraser</u>, even professionals make mistakes!

Drawing tips :

✔ while drawing with the pencil, try to use light storkes

✔ Do not rush, focus and draw slowly.

✔ Try to draw with the outline first, then the details

✔ You can always add colors to the draw

✔ Practice a lot, learning how to draw needs time to master

The Grid copy method :

The method makes drawing easier by breaking down the full image into several boxes which allows you to focus on only one box f the whole image and draw it. Begin with box A1 and work your way down to F6.

Try to focus on what is in the particular box you are working on and draw it exactly!

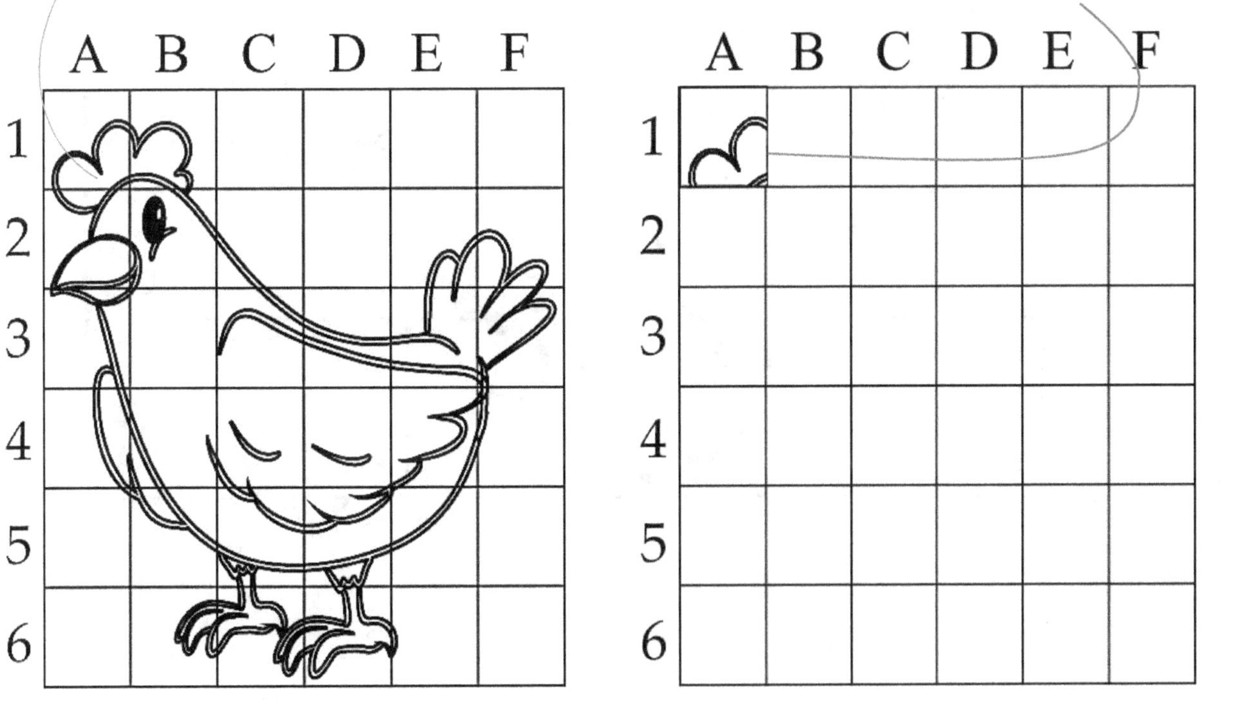

Let's draw a sheep

Now you do it!

	A	B	C	D	E	F
1						
2						
3						
4						
5						
6						

Try to trace it!

Draw it here!

Let's draw a cat

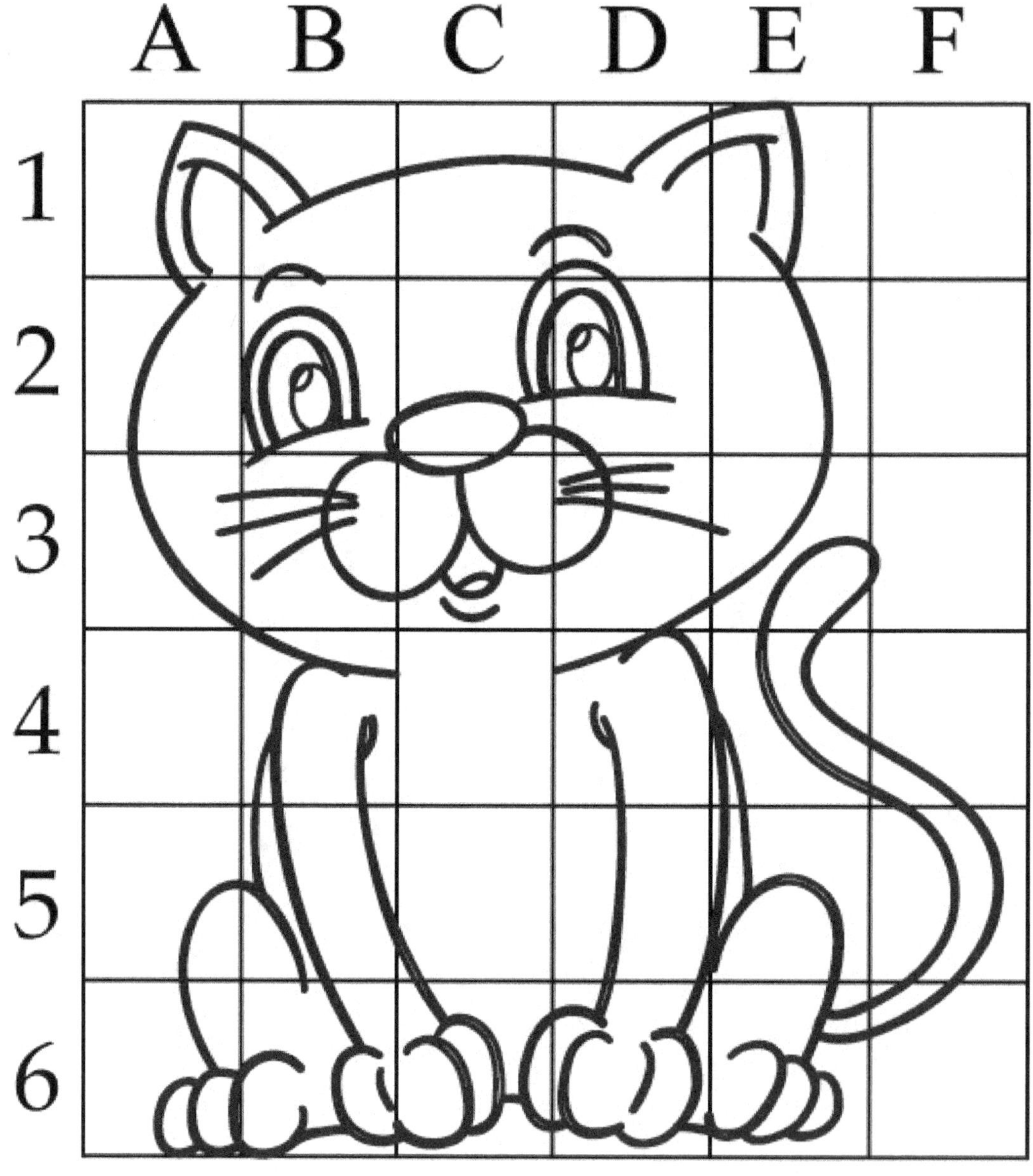

Now you do it!

	A	B	C	D	E	F
1						
2						
3						
4						
5						
6						

Try to trace it!

Draw it here!

Let's draw a chicken

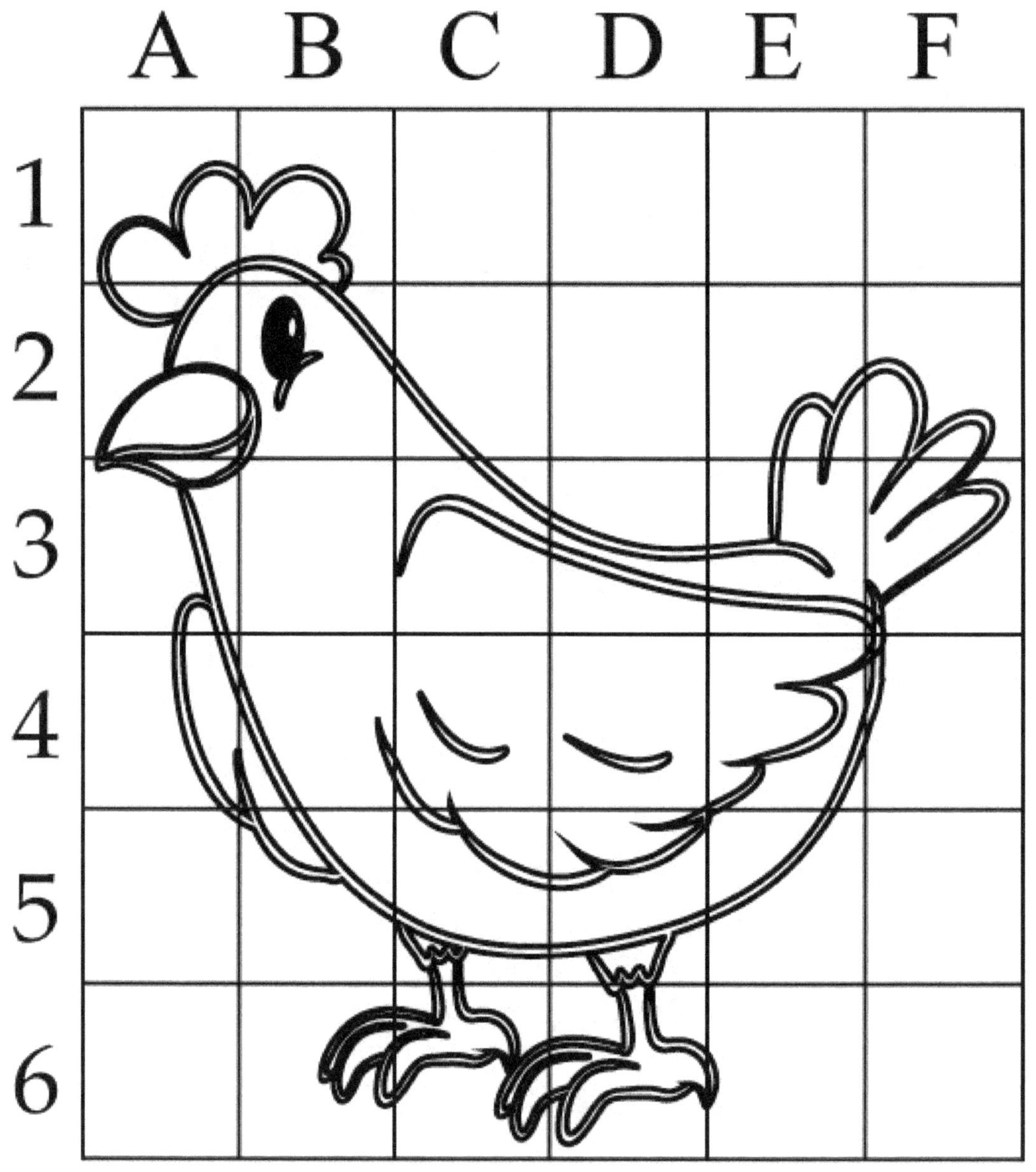

Now you do it!

	A	B	C	D	E	F
1						
2						
3						
4						
5						
6						

Try to trace it!

Draw it here!

Let's draw a flamingo

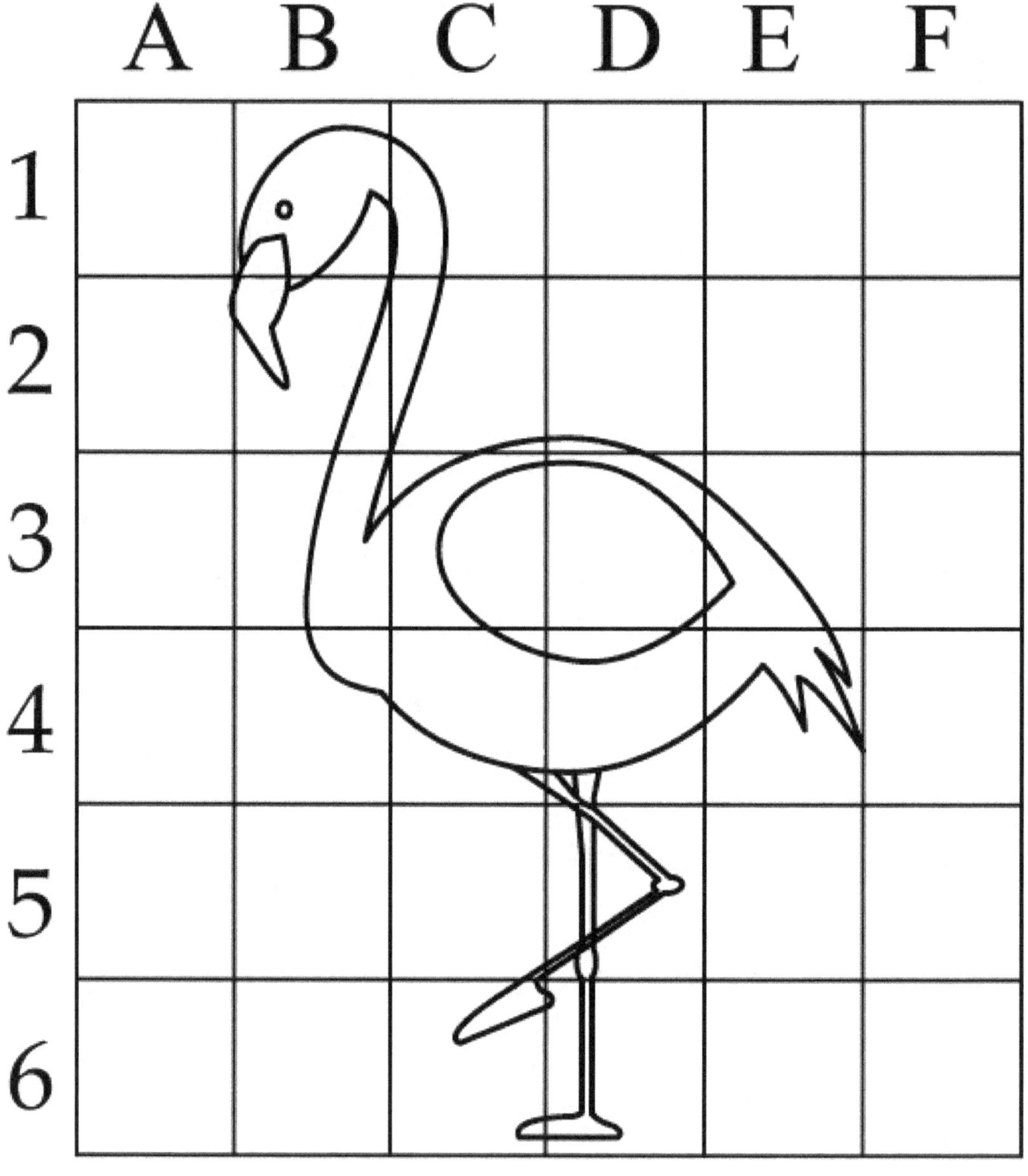

Now you do it!

	A	B	C	D	E	F
1						
2						
3						
4						
5						
6						

Try to trace it!

Draw it here!

Let's draw a lion

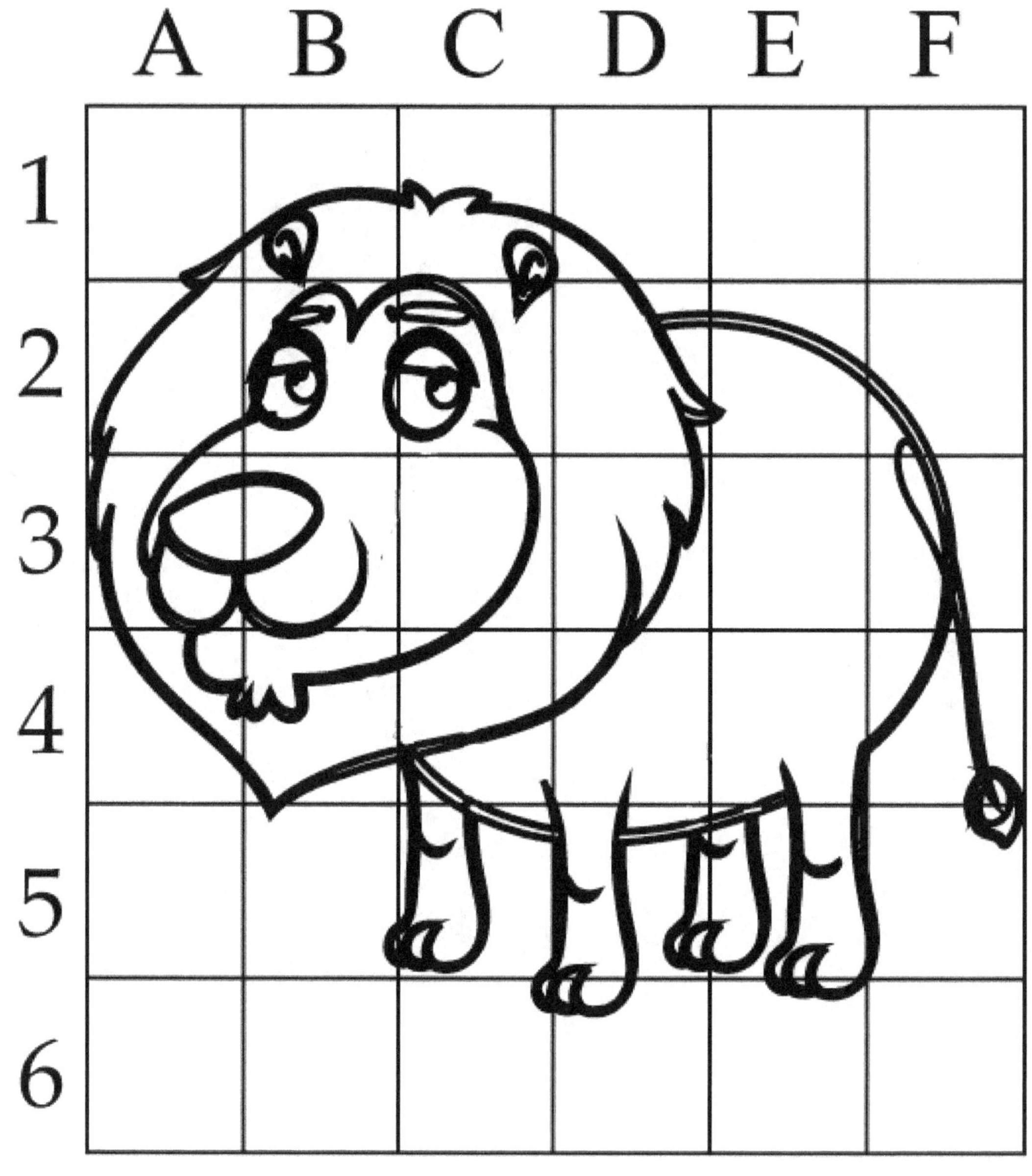

Now you do it!

	A	B	C	D	E	F
1						
2						
3						
4						
5						
6						

Try to trace it!

Draw it here!

Let's draw a fox head

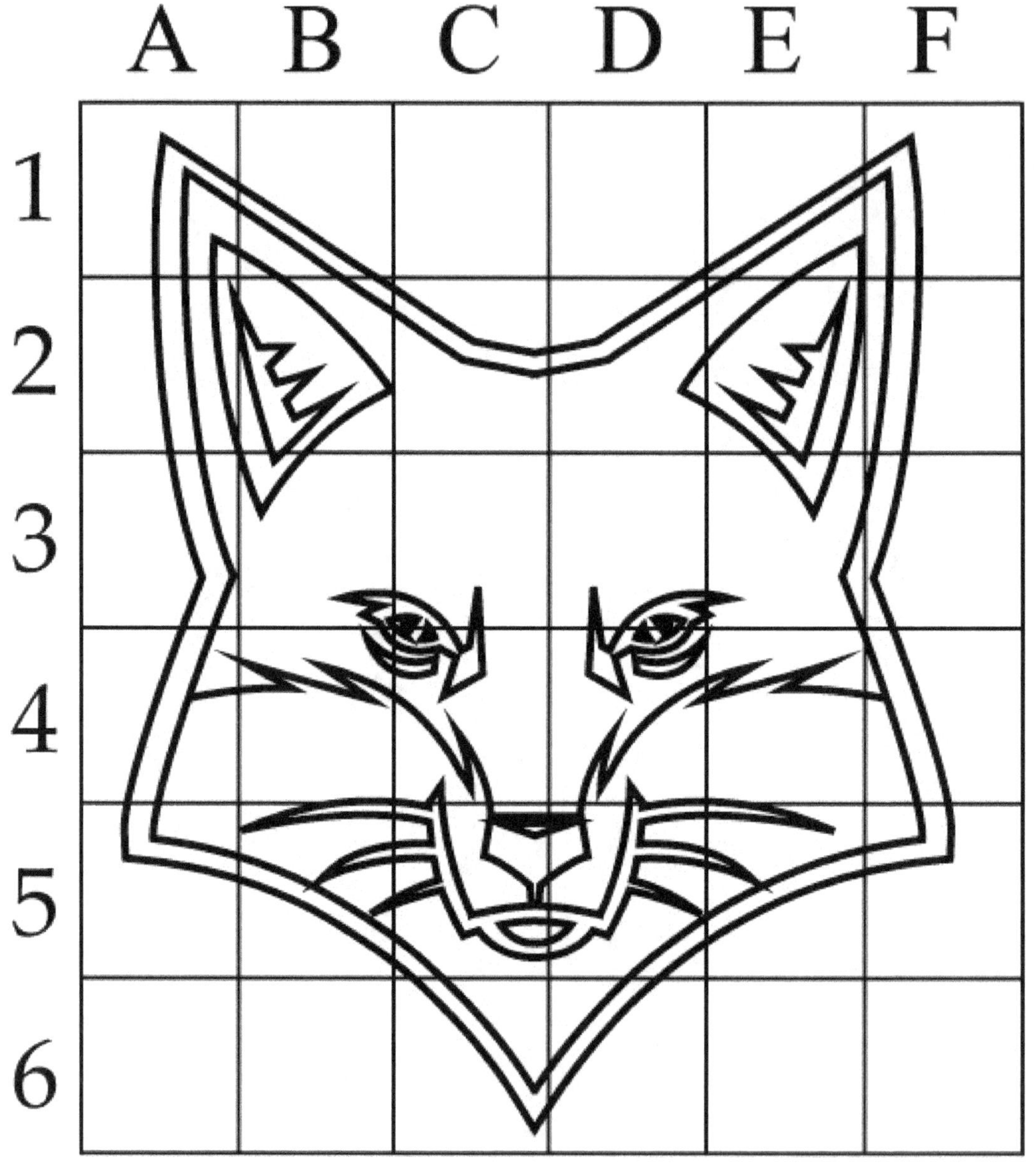

Now you do it!

	A	B	C	D	E	F
1						
2						
3						
4						
5						
6						

Try to trace it!

Draw it here!

Let's draw a dog head

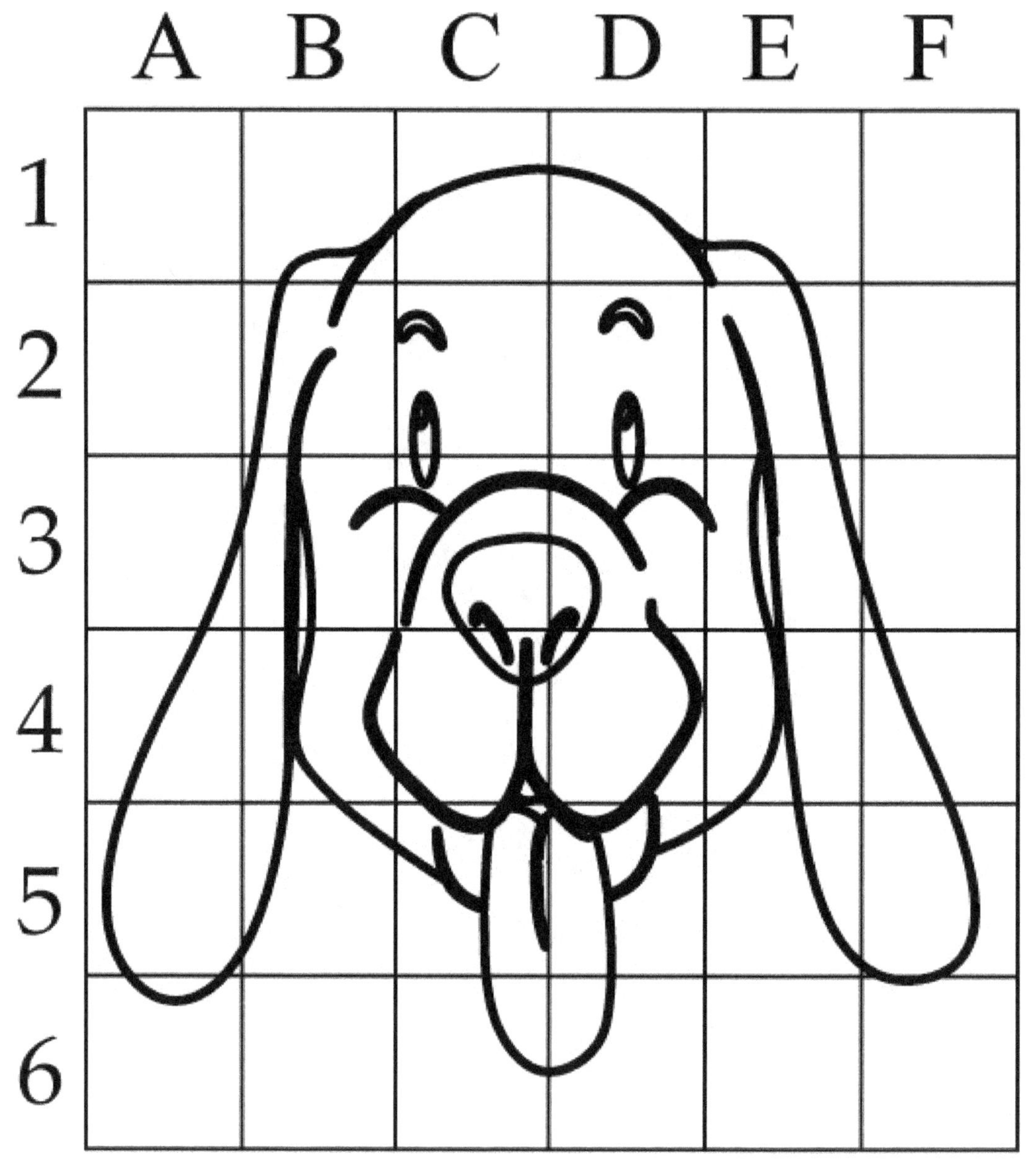

Now you do it!

	A	B	C	D	E	F
1						
2						
3						
4						
5						
6						

Try to trace it!

Draw it here!

Let's draw an elephant

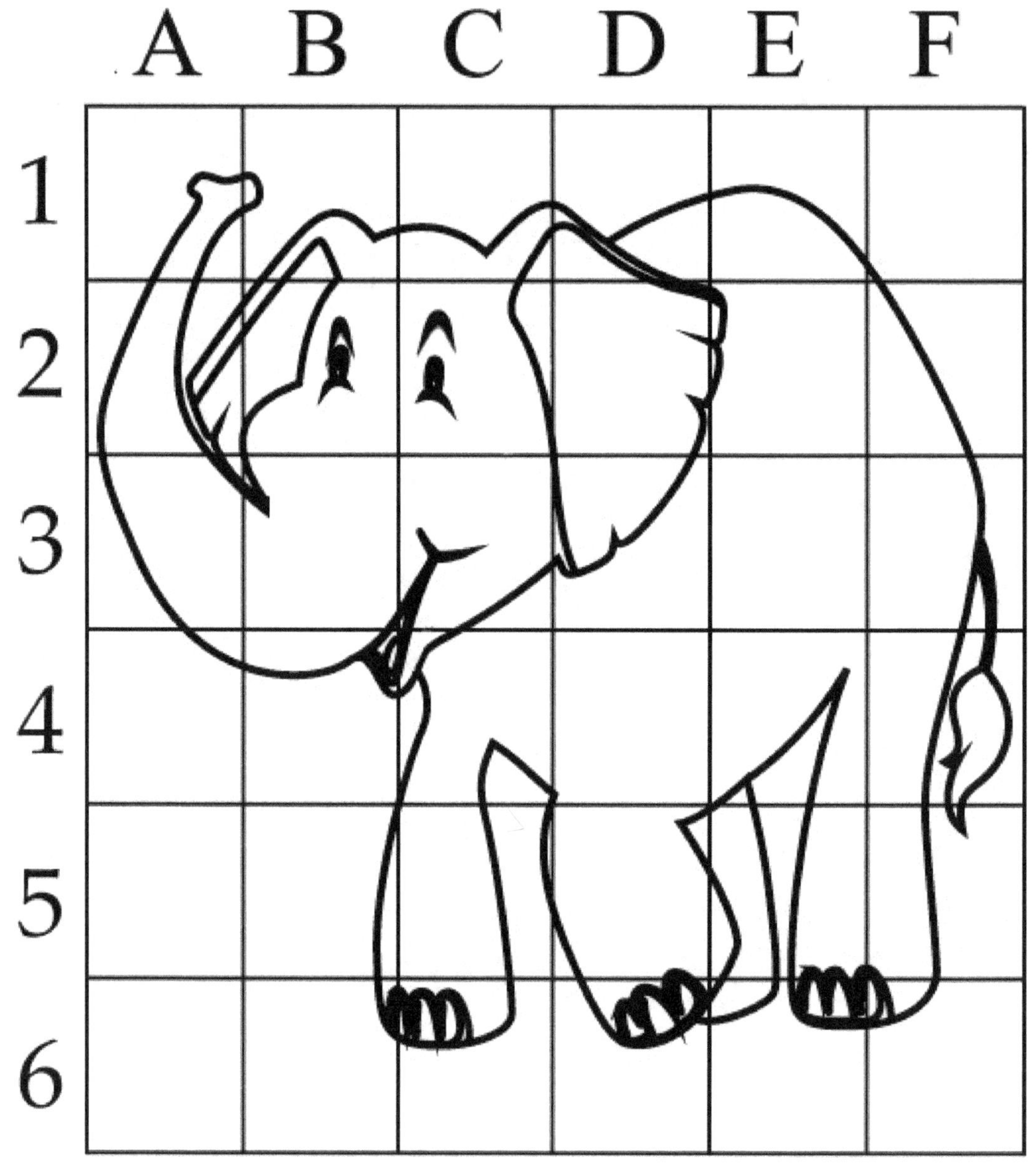

Now you do it!

	A	B	C	D	E	F
1						
2						
3						
4						
5						
6						

Try to trace it!

Draw it here!

Let's draw an owl

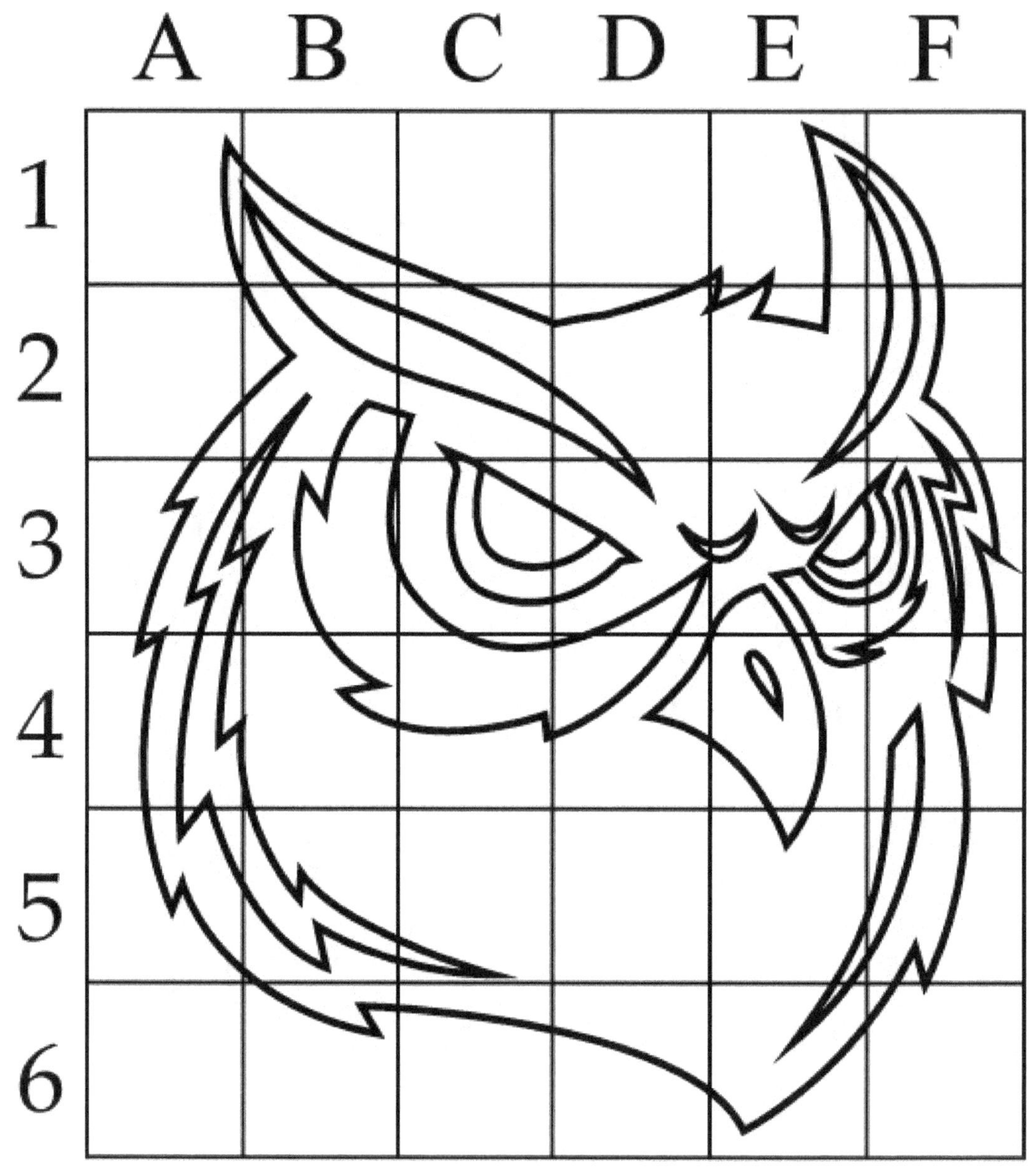

Now you do it!

	A	B	C	D	E	F
1						
2						
3						
4						
5						
6						

Try to trace it!

Draw it here!

Let's draw an eagle

Now you do it!

	A	B	C	D	E	F
1						
2						
3						
4						
5						
6						

Try to trace it!

Draw it here!

Let's draw a rabbit head

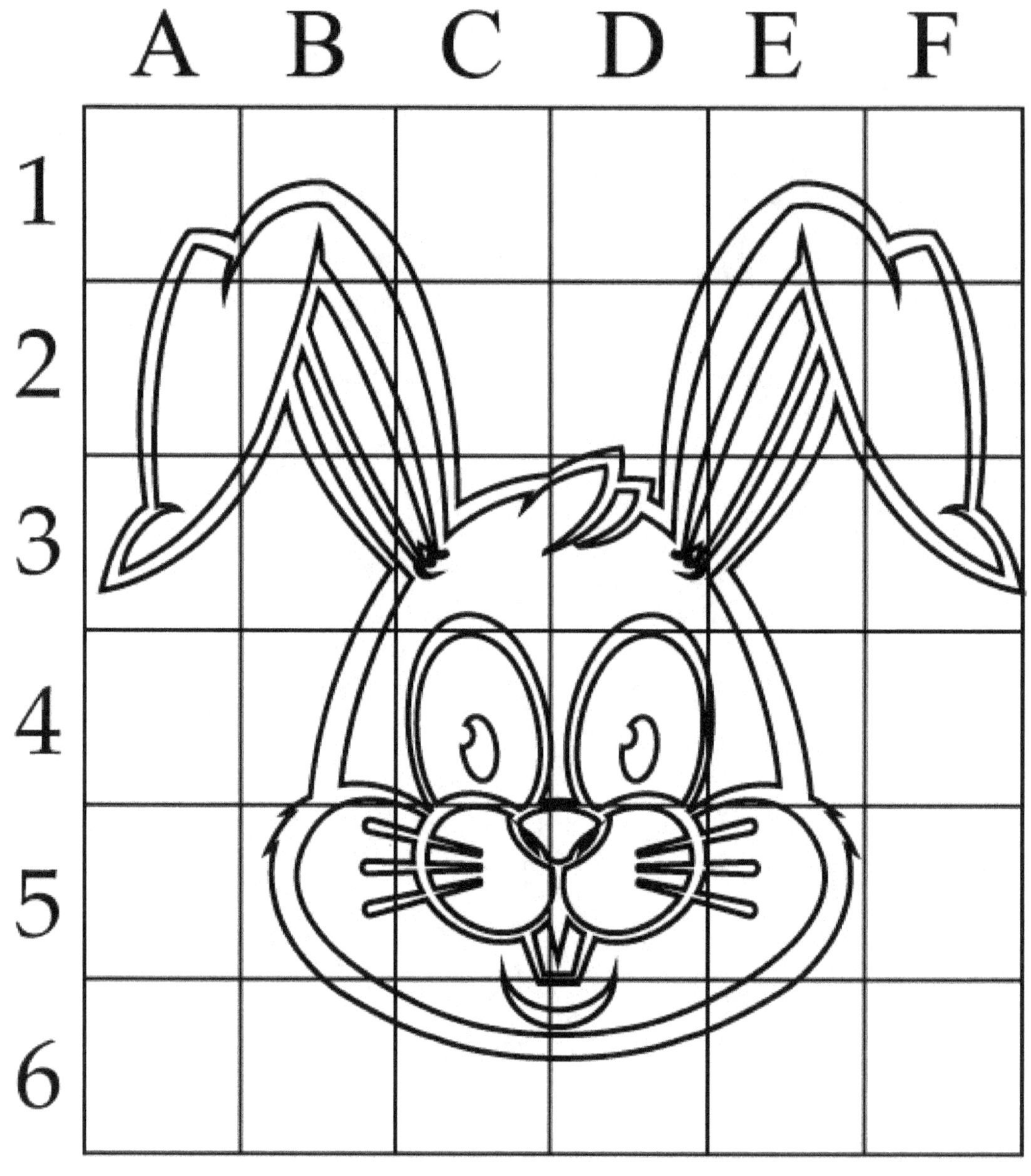

Now you do it!

	A	B	C	D	E	F
1						
2						
3						
4						
5						
6						

Try to trace it!

Draw it here!

Let's draw a frog

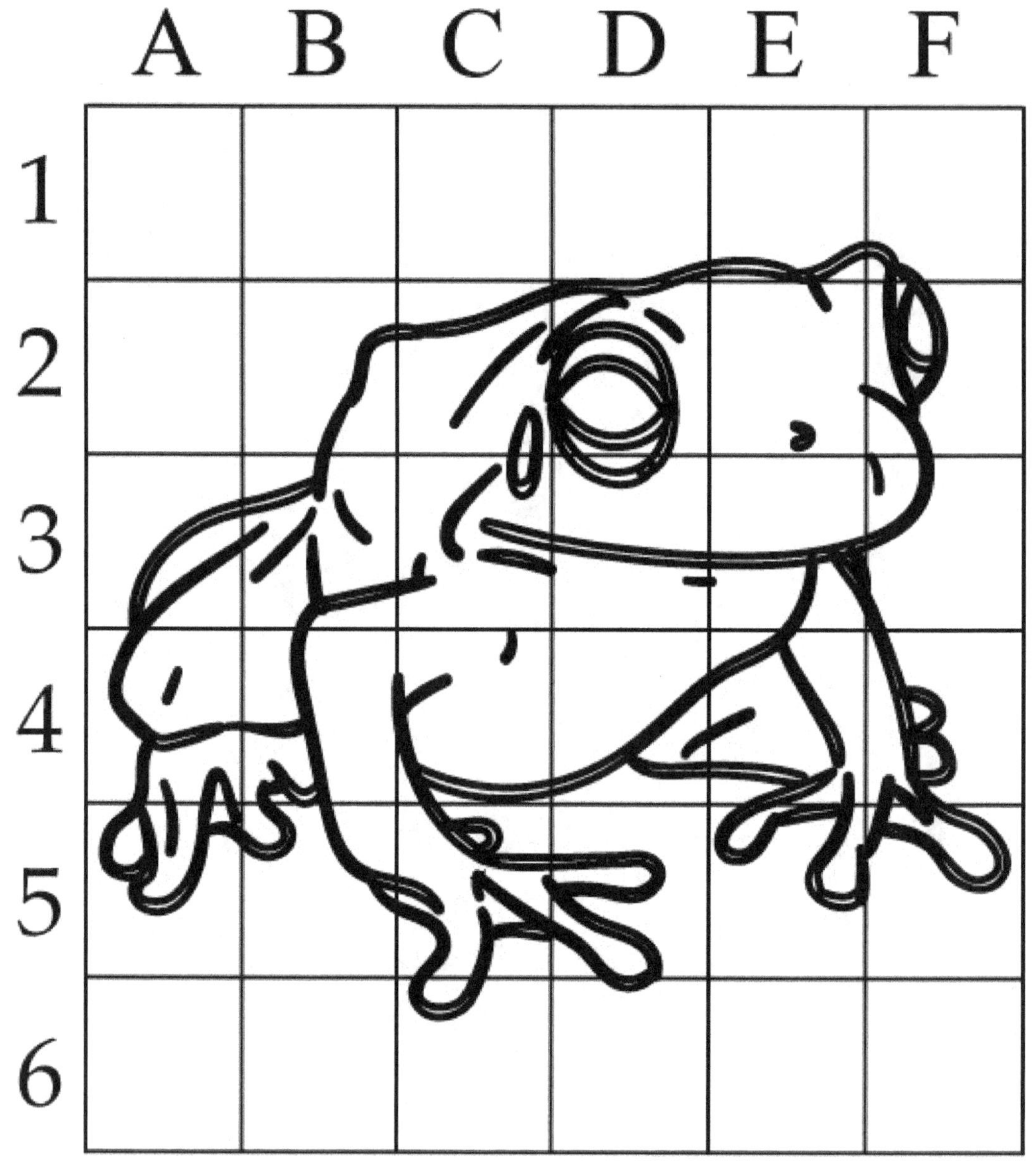

Now you do it!

	A	B	C	D	E	F
1						
2						
3						
4						
5						
6						

Try to trace it!

Draw it here!

Let's draw a camel

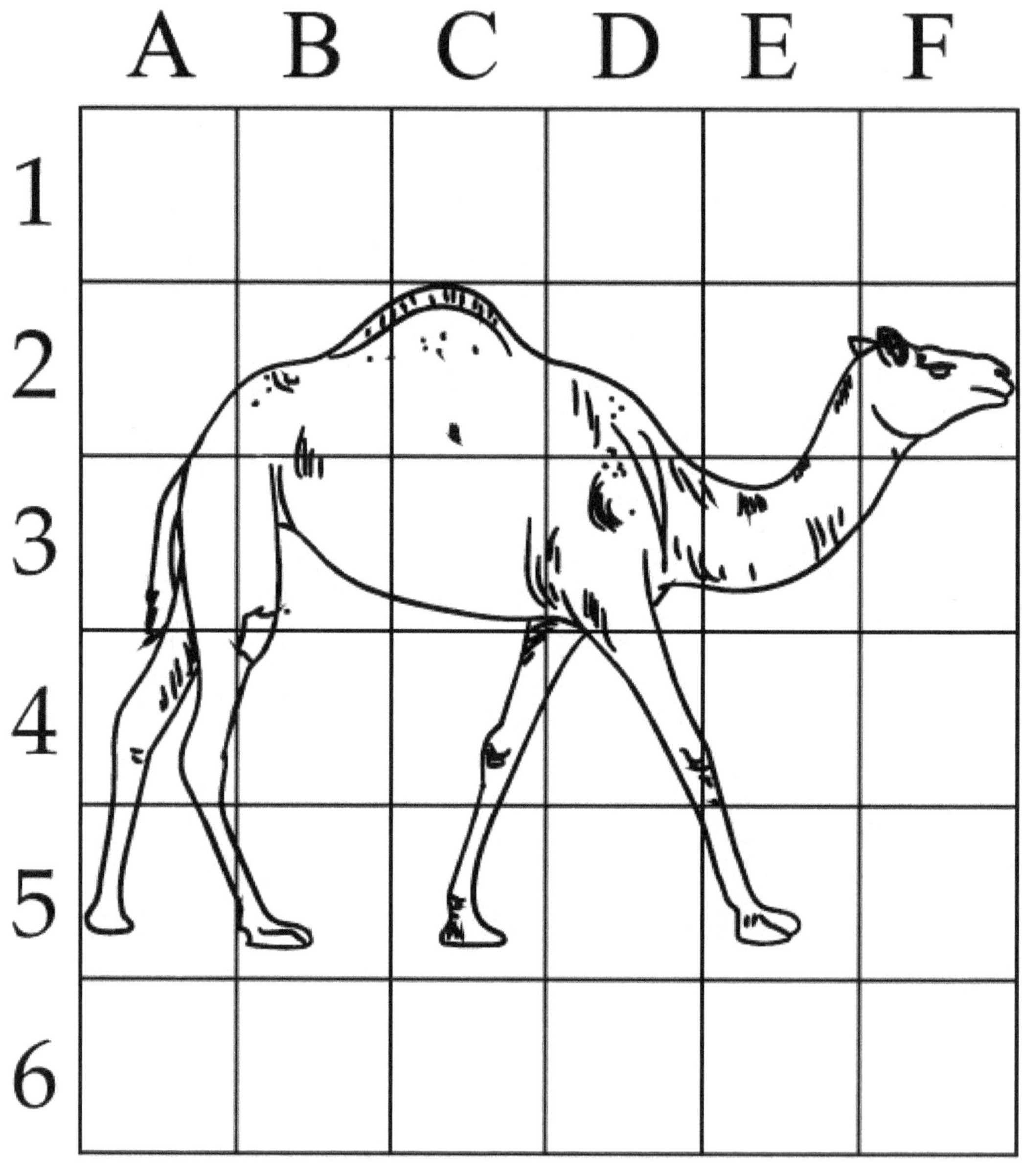

Now you do it!

	A	B	C	D	E	F
1						
2						
3						
4						
5						
6						

Try to trace it!

Draw it here!

Let's draw a giraffe

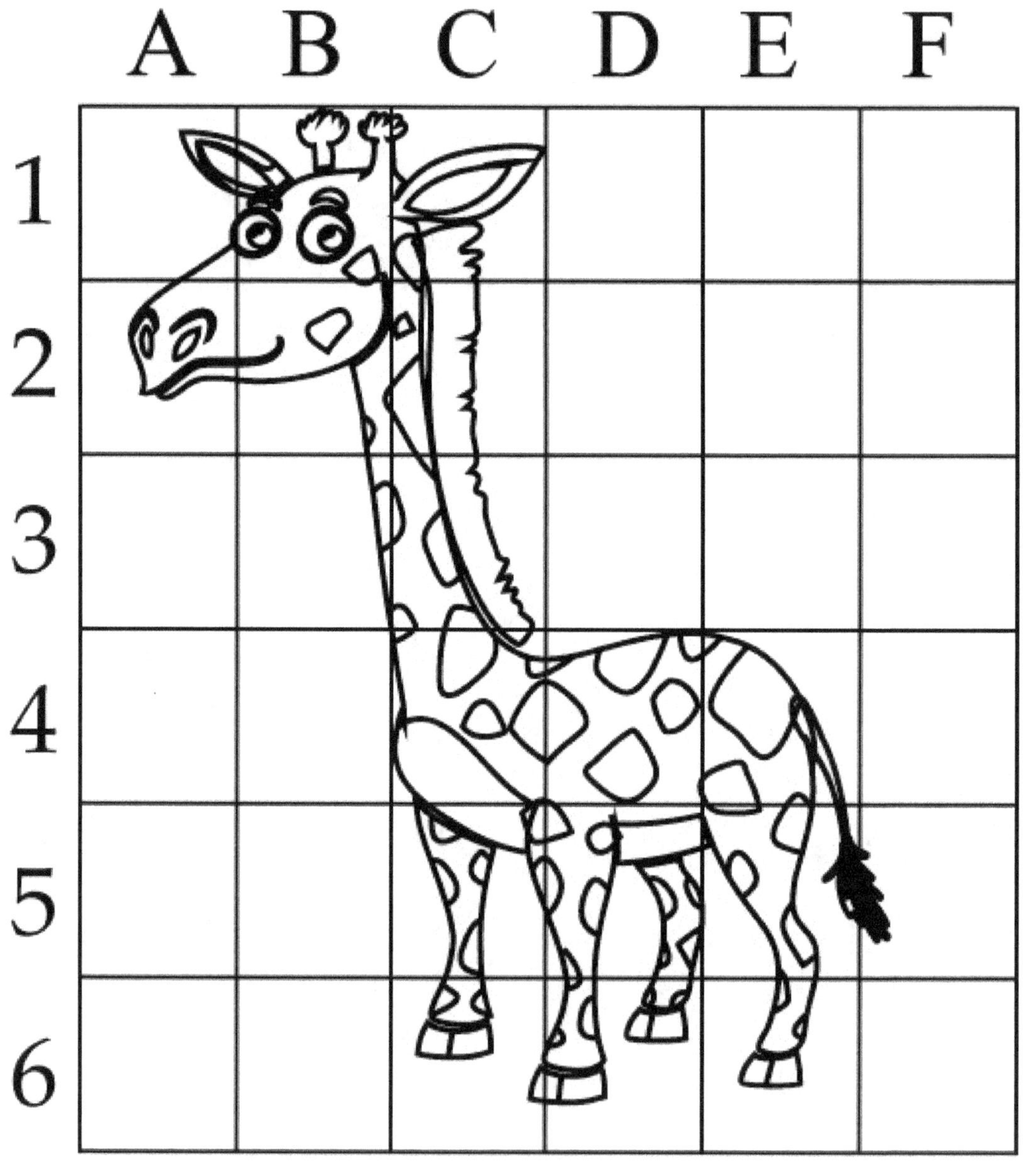

Now you do it!

	A	B	C	D	E	F
1						
2						
3						
4						
5						
6						

Try to trace it!

Draw it here!

Let's draw a cow

Now you do it!

	A	B	C	D	E	F
1						
2						
3						
4						
5						
6						

Try to trace it!

Draw it here!

Let's draw a reindeer head

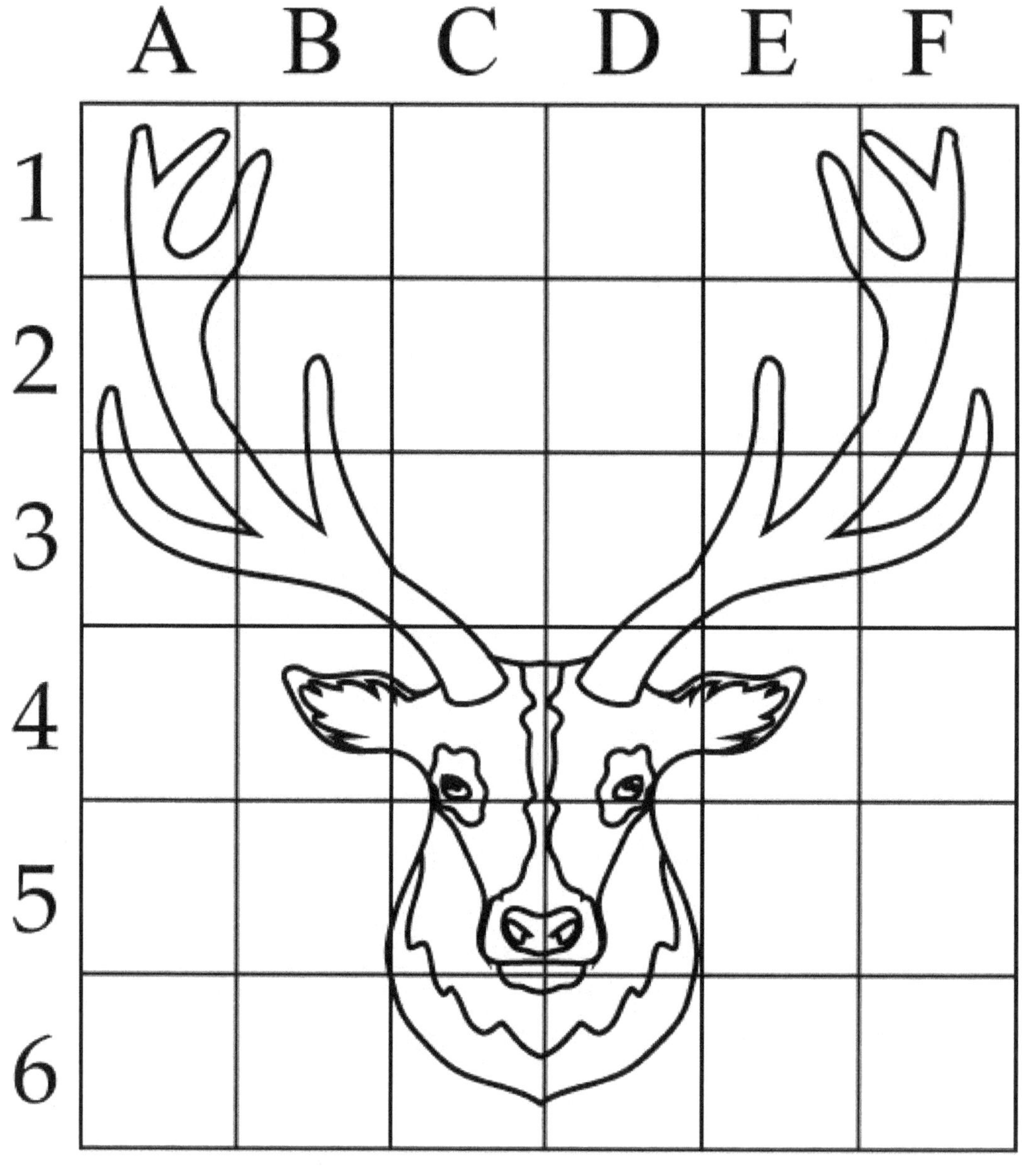

Now you do it!

	A	B	C	D	E	F
1						
2						
3						
4						
5						
6						

Try to trace it!

Draw it here!

Let's draw a unicorn

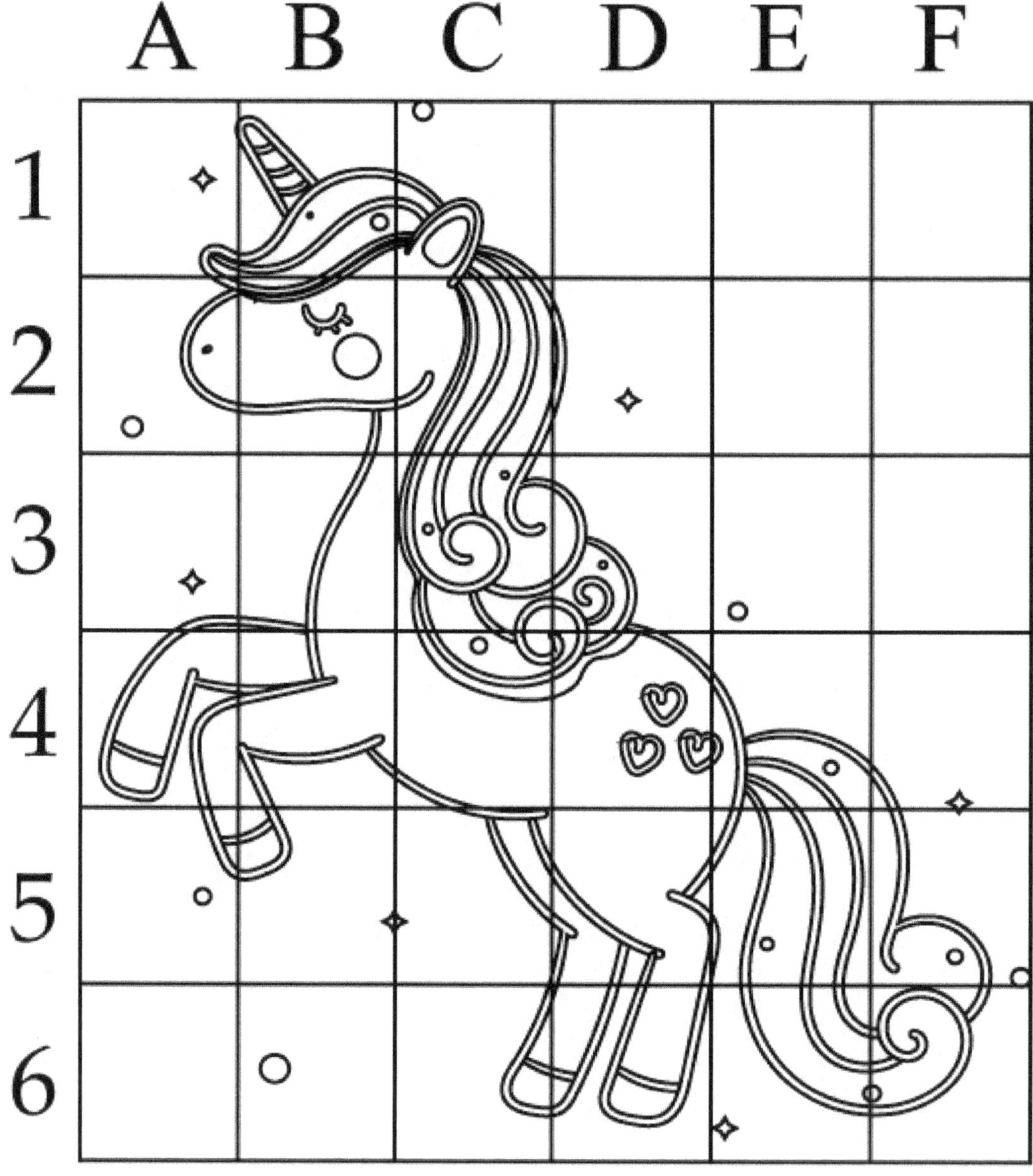

Now you do it!

	A	B	C	D	E	F
1						
2						
3						
4						
5						
6						

Try to trace it!

Draw it here!

Let's draw an elf

Now you do it!

	A	B	C	D	E	F
1						
2						
3						
4						
5						
6						

Try to trace it!

Draw it here!

Let's draw a snowman

Now you do it!

	A	B	C	D	E	F
1						
2						
3						
4						
5						
6						

Try to trace it!

Draw it here!

Let's draw a fairy

Now you do it!

	A	B	C	D	E	F
1						
2						
3						
4						
5						
6						

Try to trace it!

Draw it here!

Let's draw a santa claus head

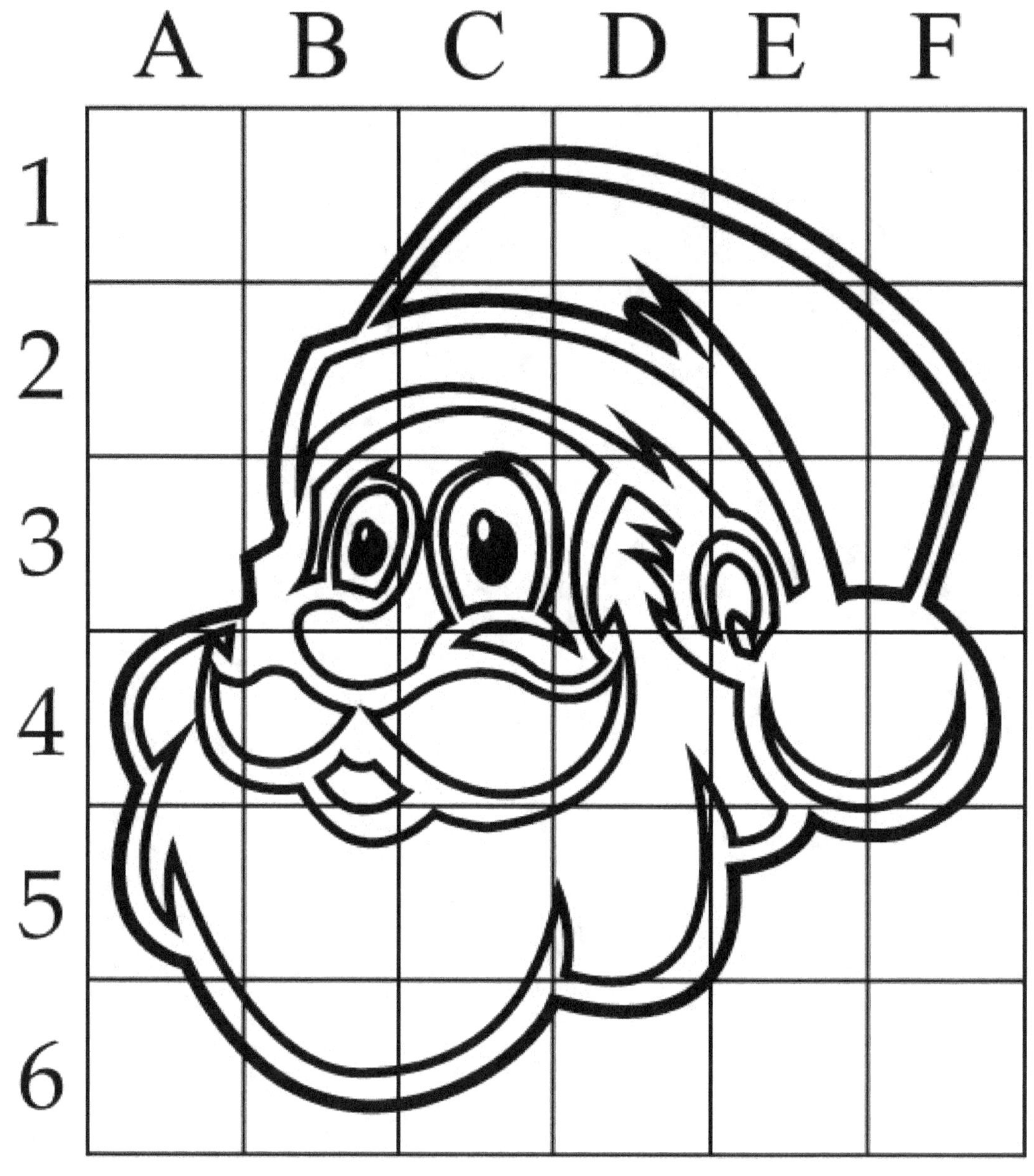

Now you do it!

	A	B	C	D	E	F
1						
2						
3						
4						
5						
6						

Try to trace it!

Draw it here!

Let's draw a dragon

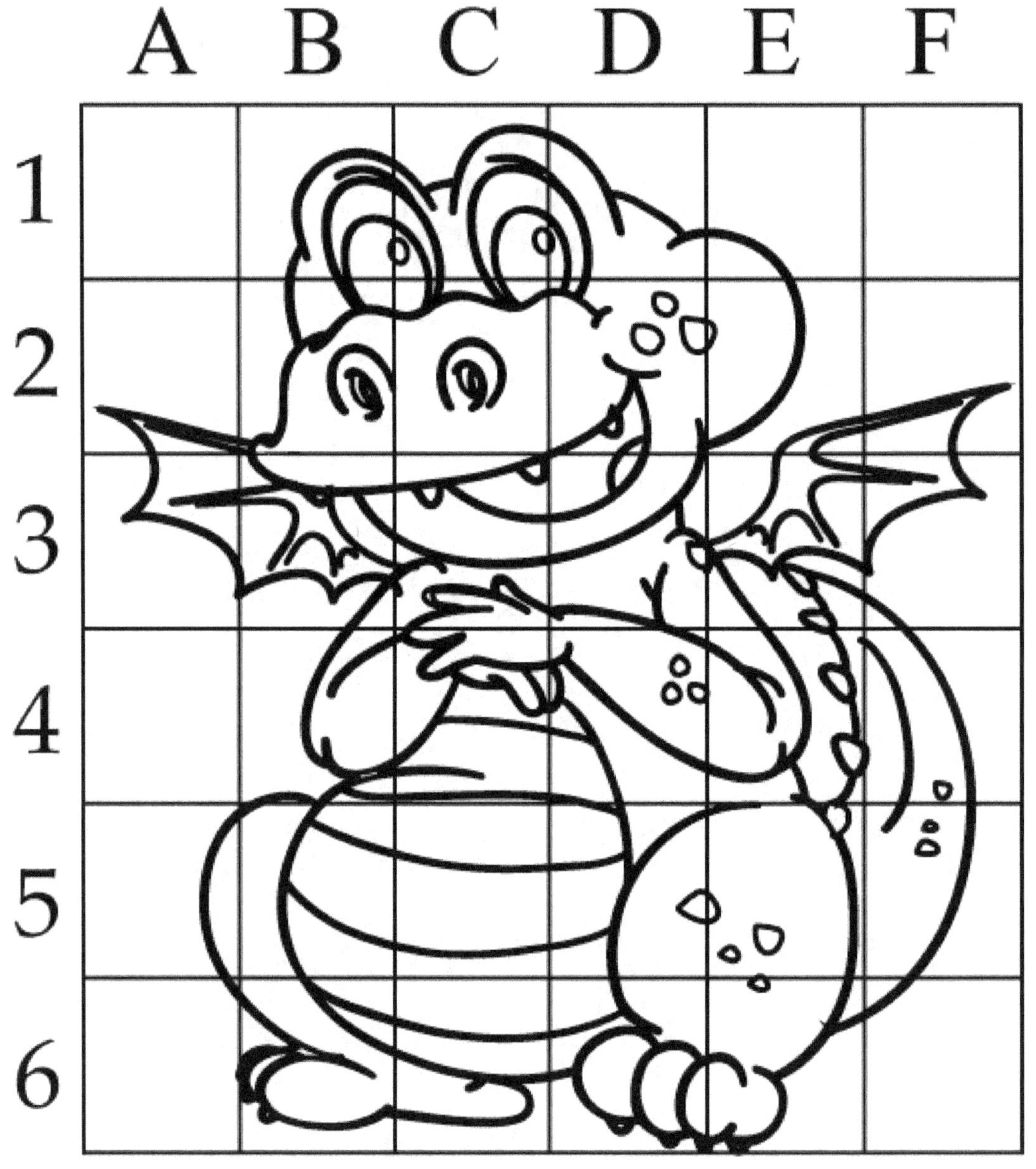

Now you do it!

	A	B	C	D	E	F
1						
2						
3						
4						
5						
6						

Try to trace it!

Draw it here!

Let's draw a fish

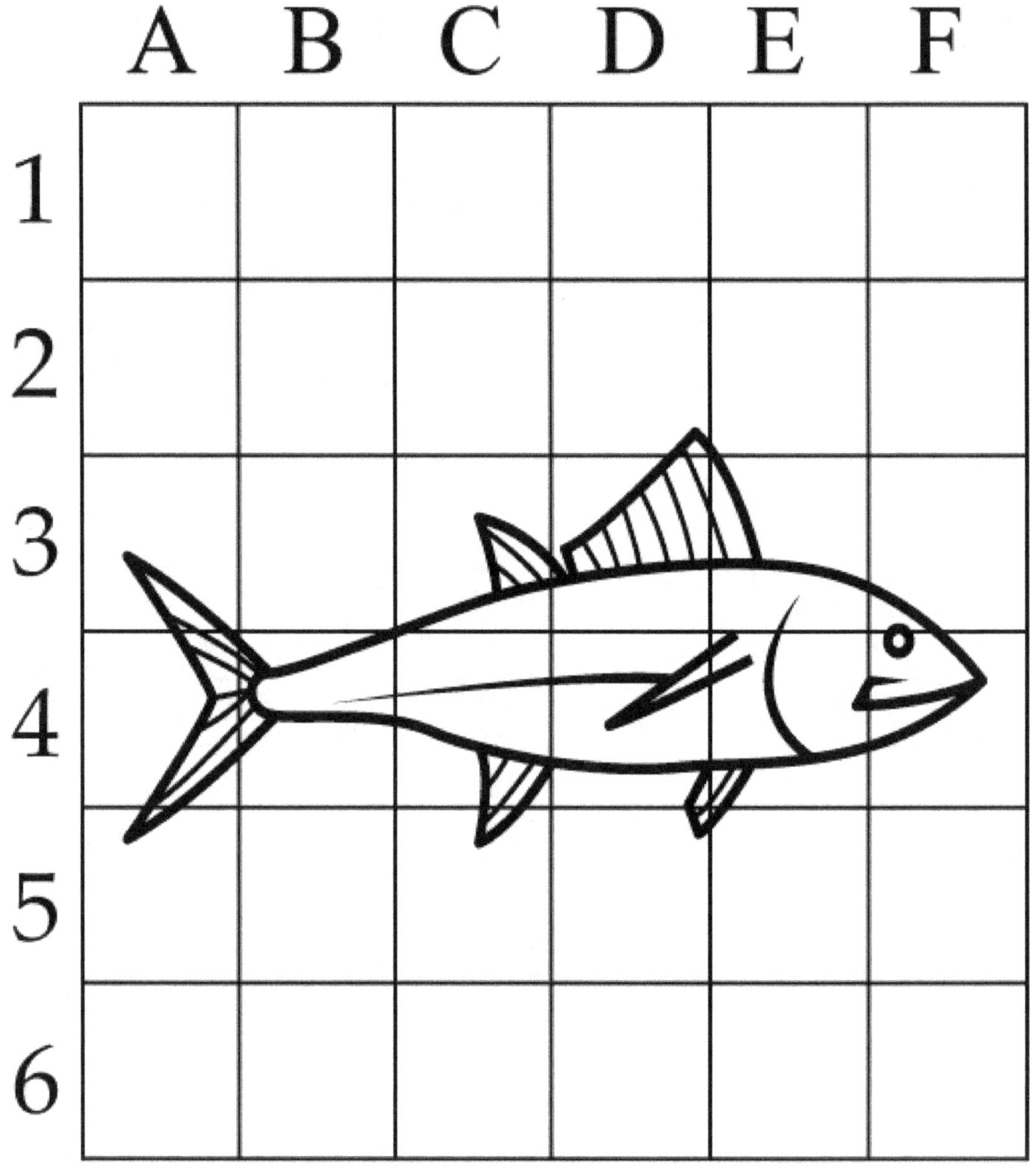

Now you do it!

	A	B	C	D	E	F
1						
2						
3						
4						
5						
6						

Try to trace it!

Draw it here!

Let's draw a swordfish

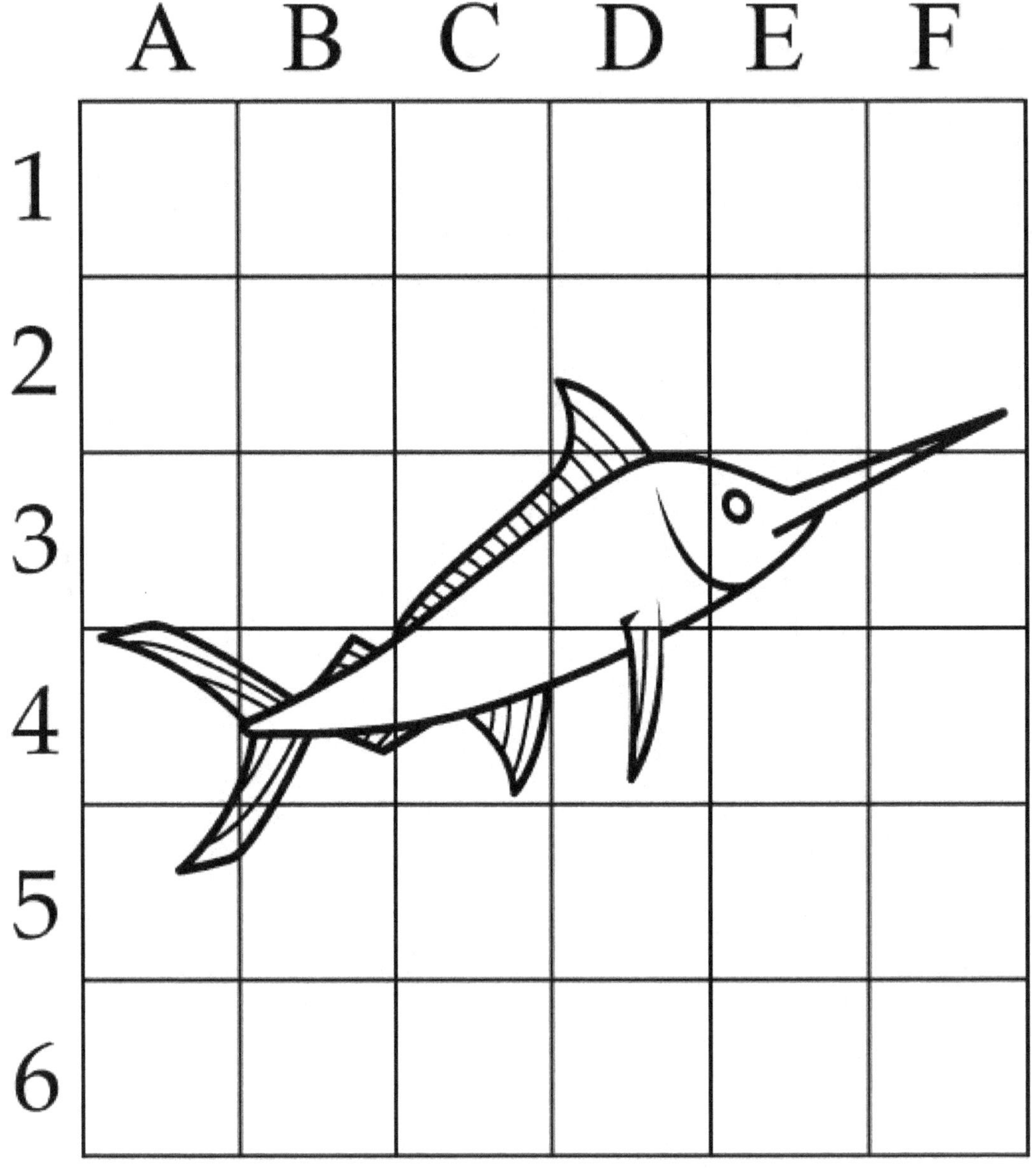

Now you do it!

	A	B	C	D	E	F
1						
2						
3						
4						
5						
6						

Try to trace it!

Draw it here!

Let's draw a shark

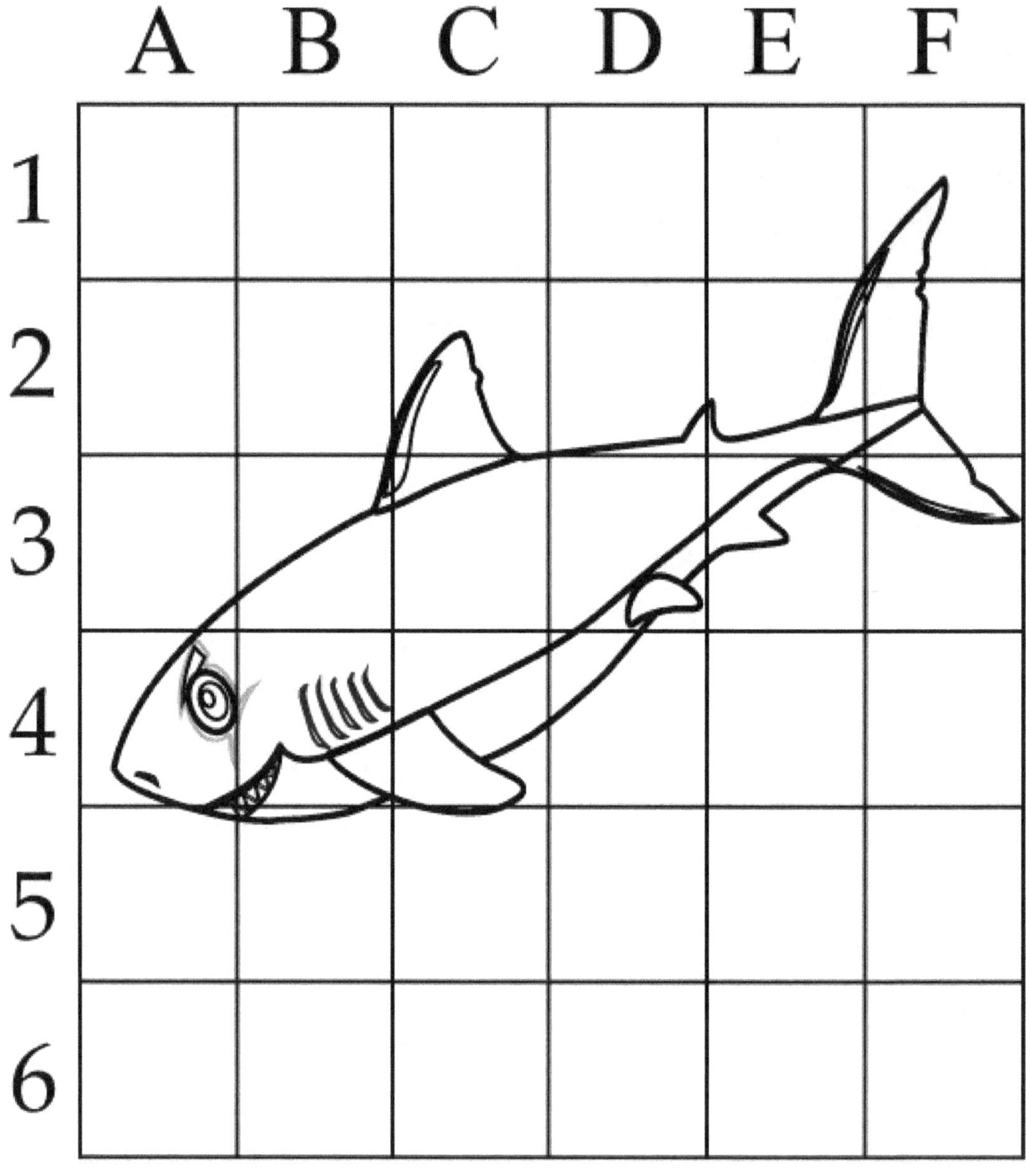

Now you do it!

	A	B	C	D	E	F
1						
2						
3						
4						
5						
6						

Try to trace it!

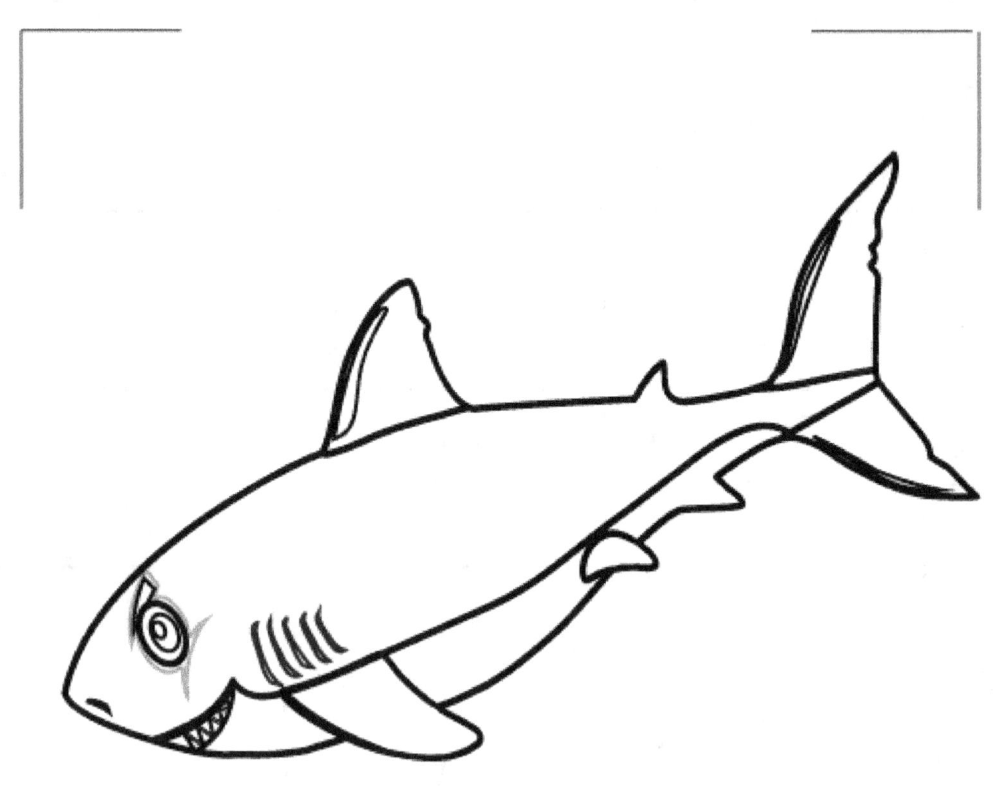

Draw it here!

Let's draw a whale

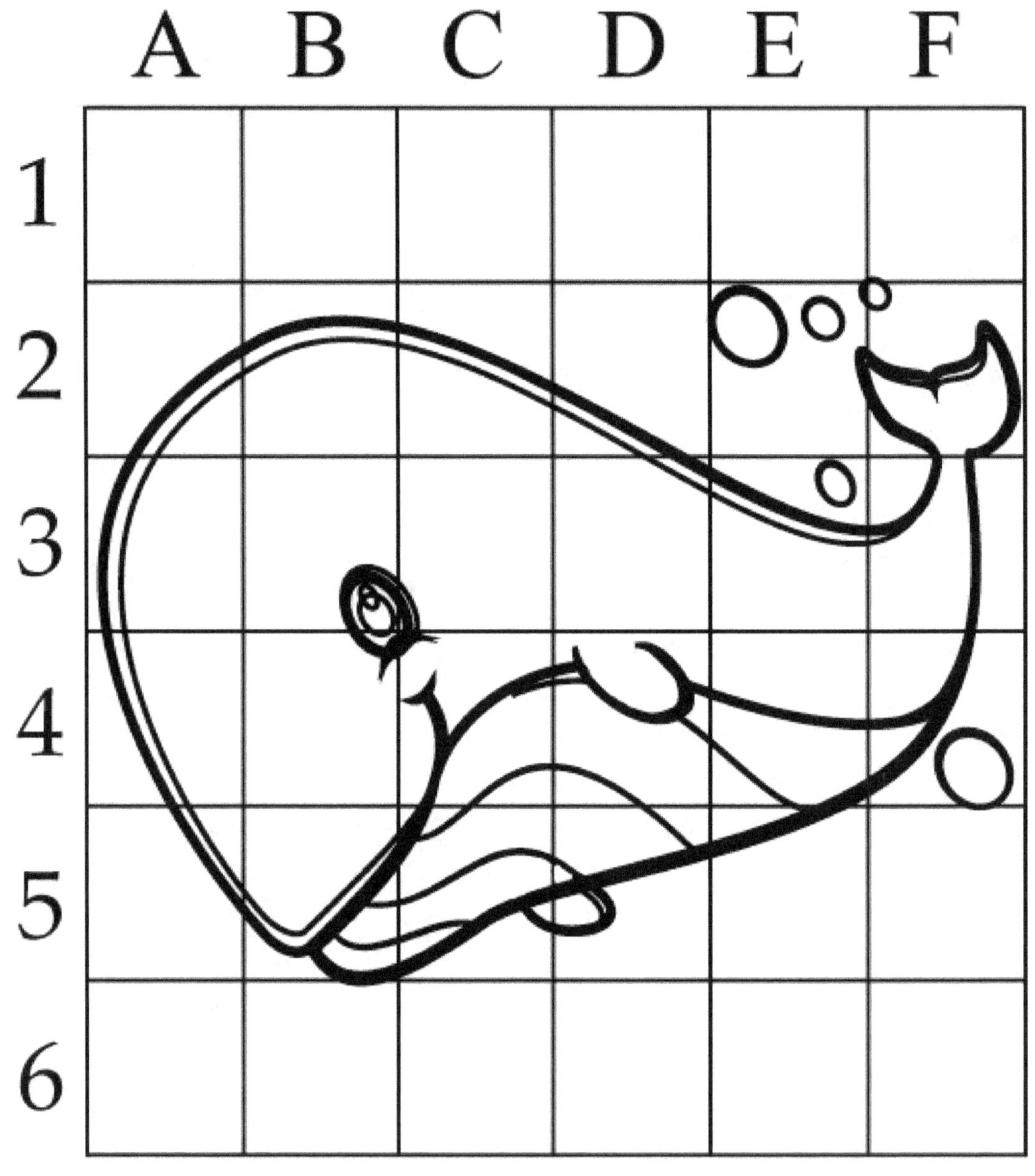

Now you do it!

	A	B	C	D	E	F
1						
2						
3						
4						
5						
6						

Try to trace it!

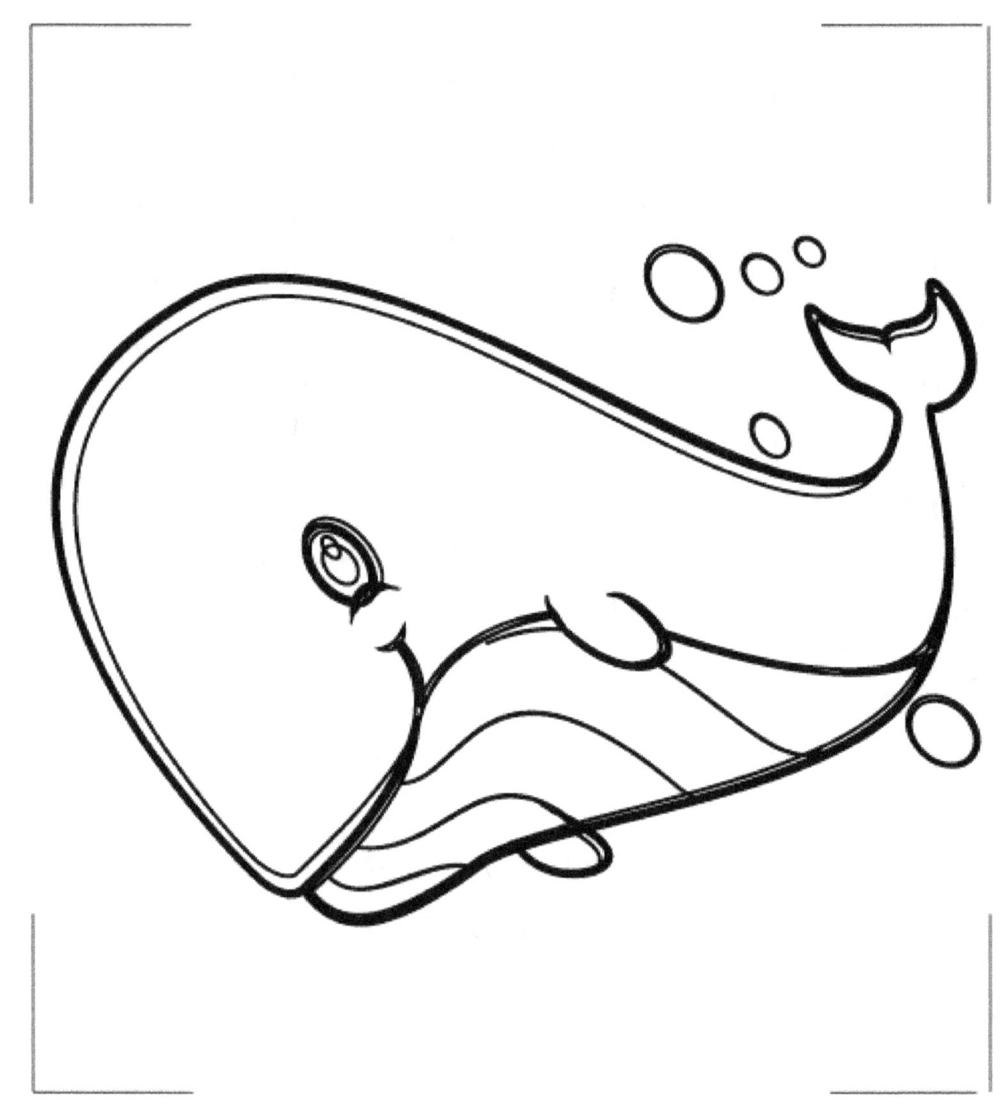

Draw it here!

Let's draw a penguin

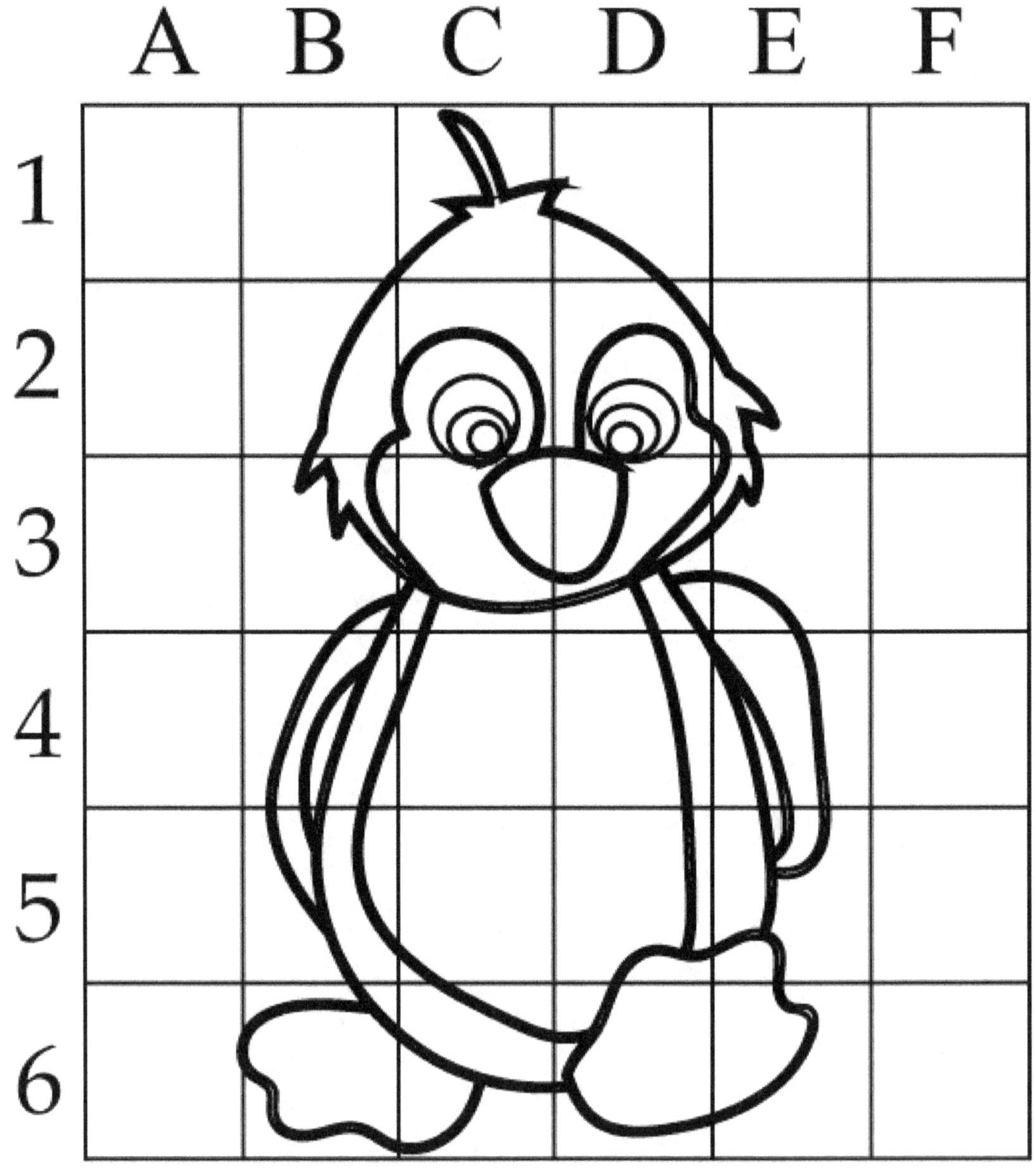

Now you do it!

	A	B	C	D	E	F
1						
2						
3						
4						
5						
6						

Try to trace it!

Draw it here!

Let's draw a seahorse

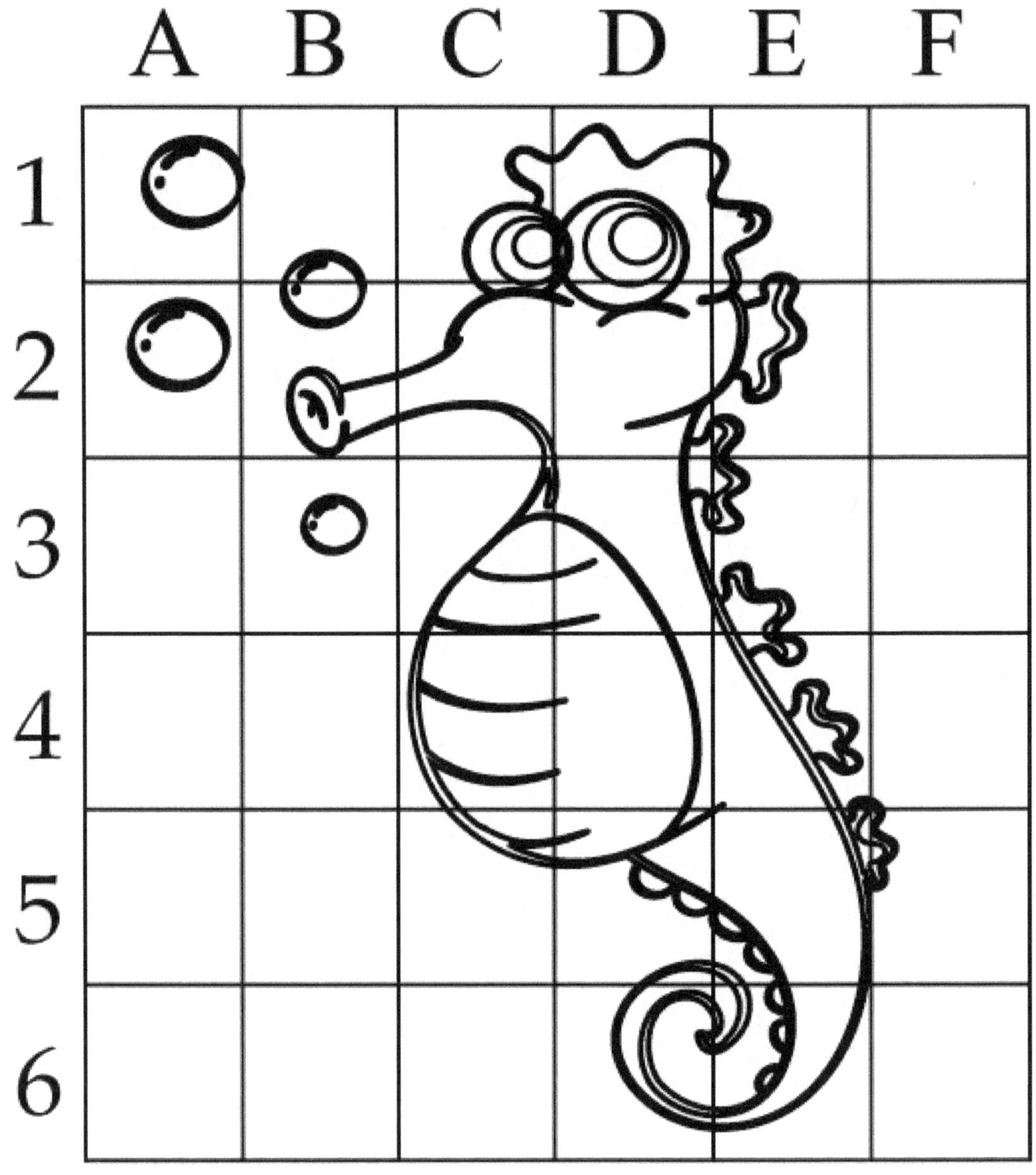

Now you do it!

	A	B	C	D	E	F
1						
2						
3						
4						
5						
6						

Try to trace it!

Draw it here!

Let's draw an octopus

Now you do it!

	A	B	C	D	E	F
1						
2						
3						
4						
5						
6						

Try to trace it!

Draw it here!

Let's draw a teddy bear

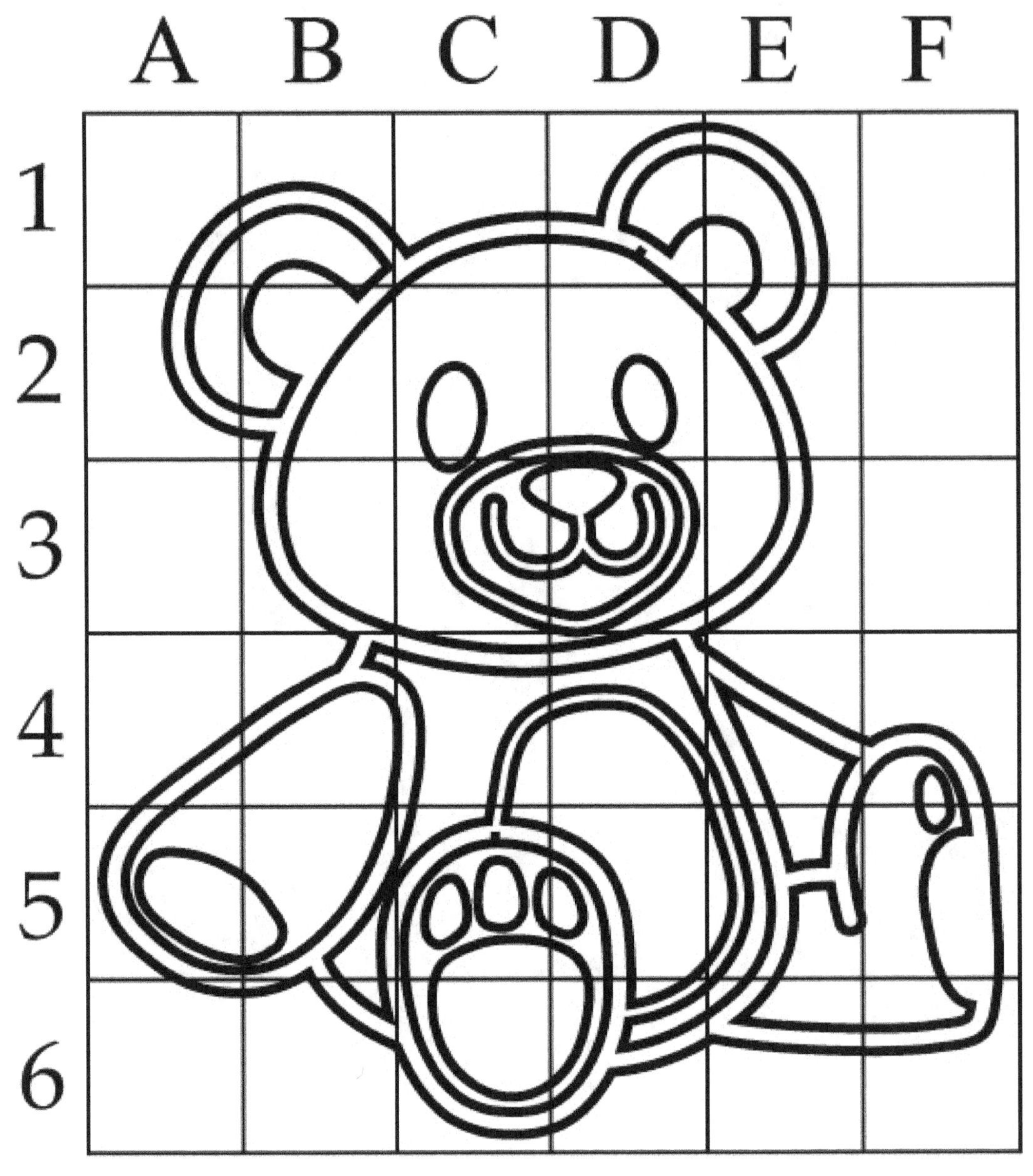

Now you do it!

	A	B	C	D	E	F
1						
2						
3						
4						
5						
6						

Try to trace it!

Draw it here!

Let's draw a birthday cake

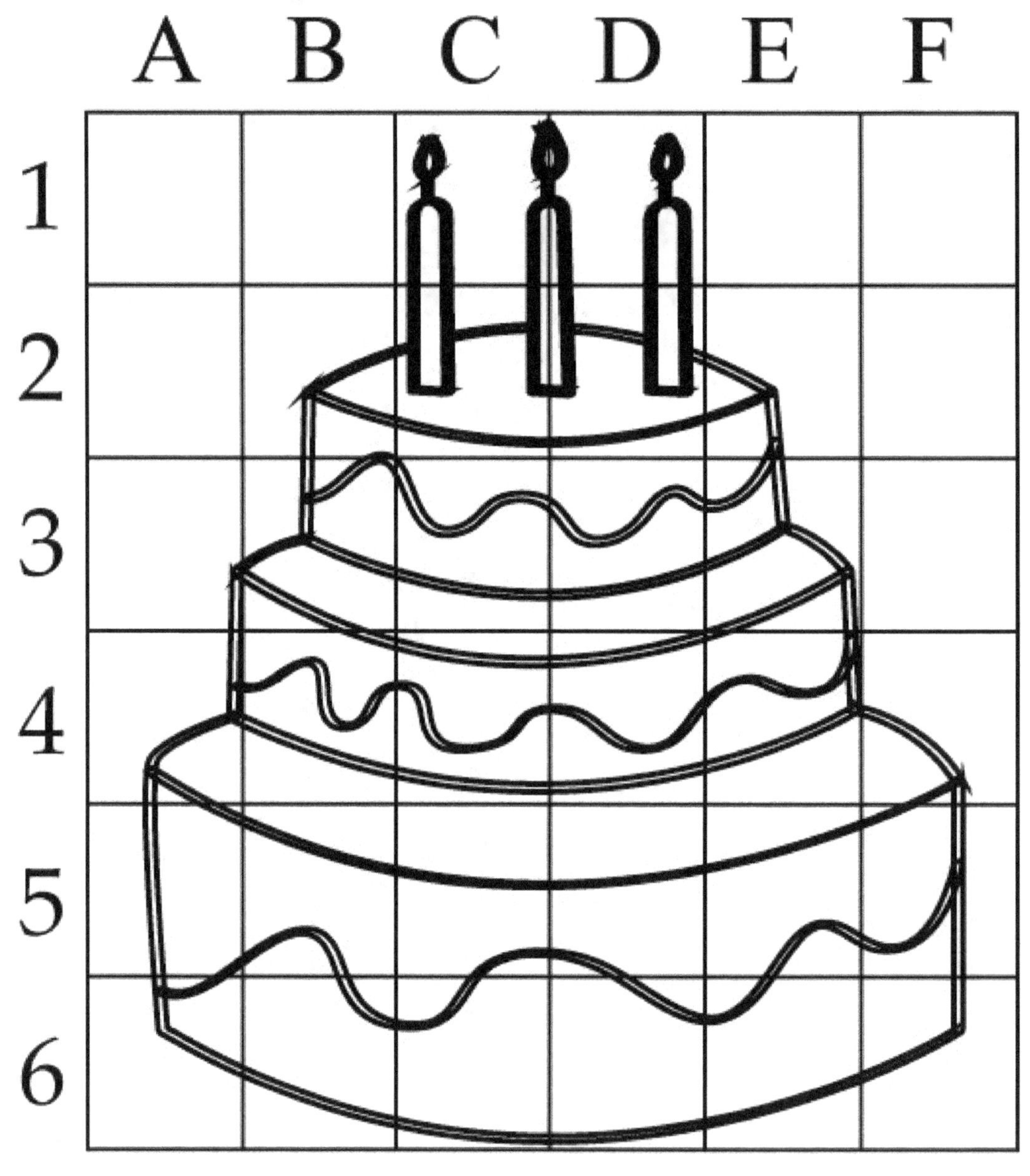

Now you do it!

	A	B	C	D	E	F
1						
2						
3						
4						
5						
6						

Try to trace it!

Draw it here!

Let's draw a tree

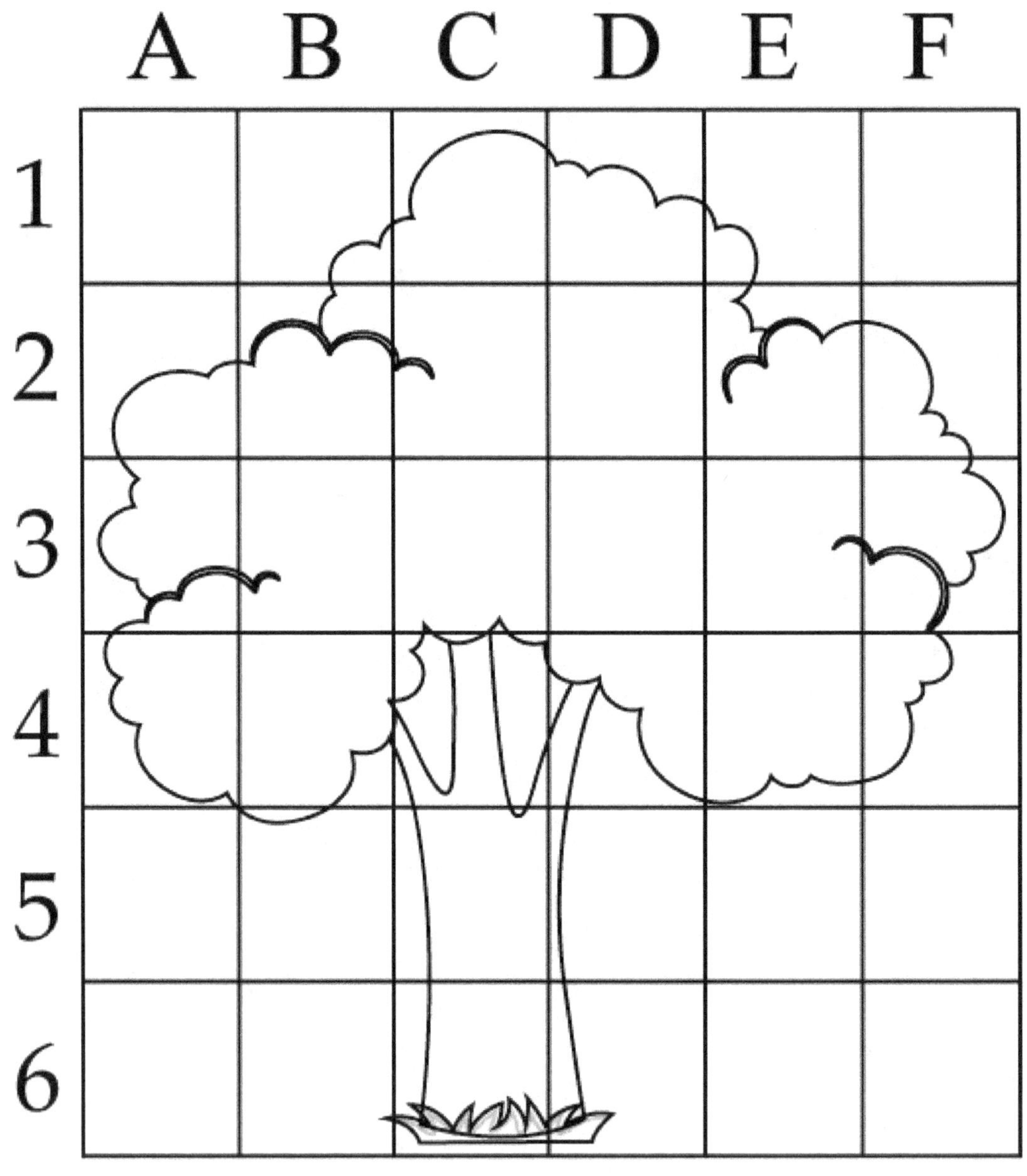

Now you do it!

	A	B	C	D	E	F
1						
2						
3						
4						
5						
6						

Try to trace it!

Draw it here!

Let's draw a house

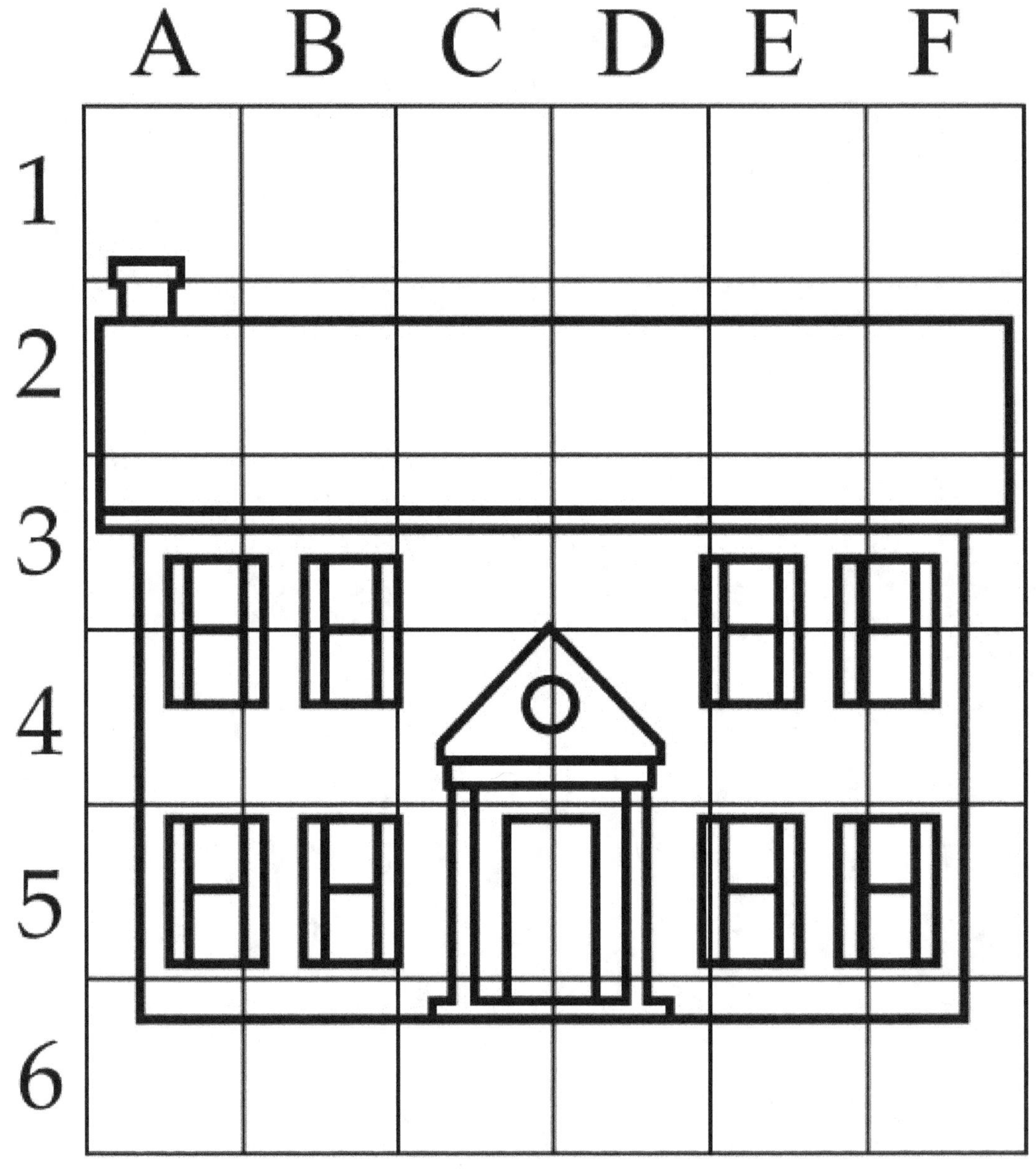

Now you do it!

	A	B	C	D	E	F
1						
2						
3						
4						
5						
6						

Try to trace it!

Draw it here!

Let's draw a christmas tree

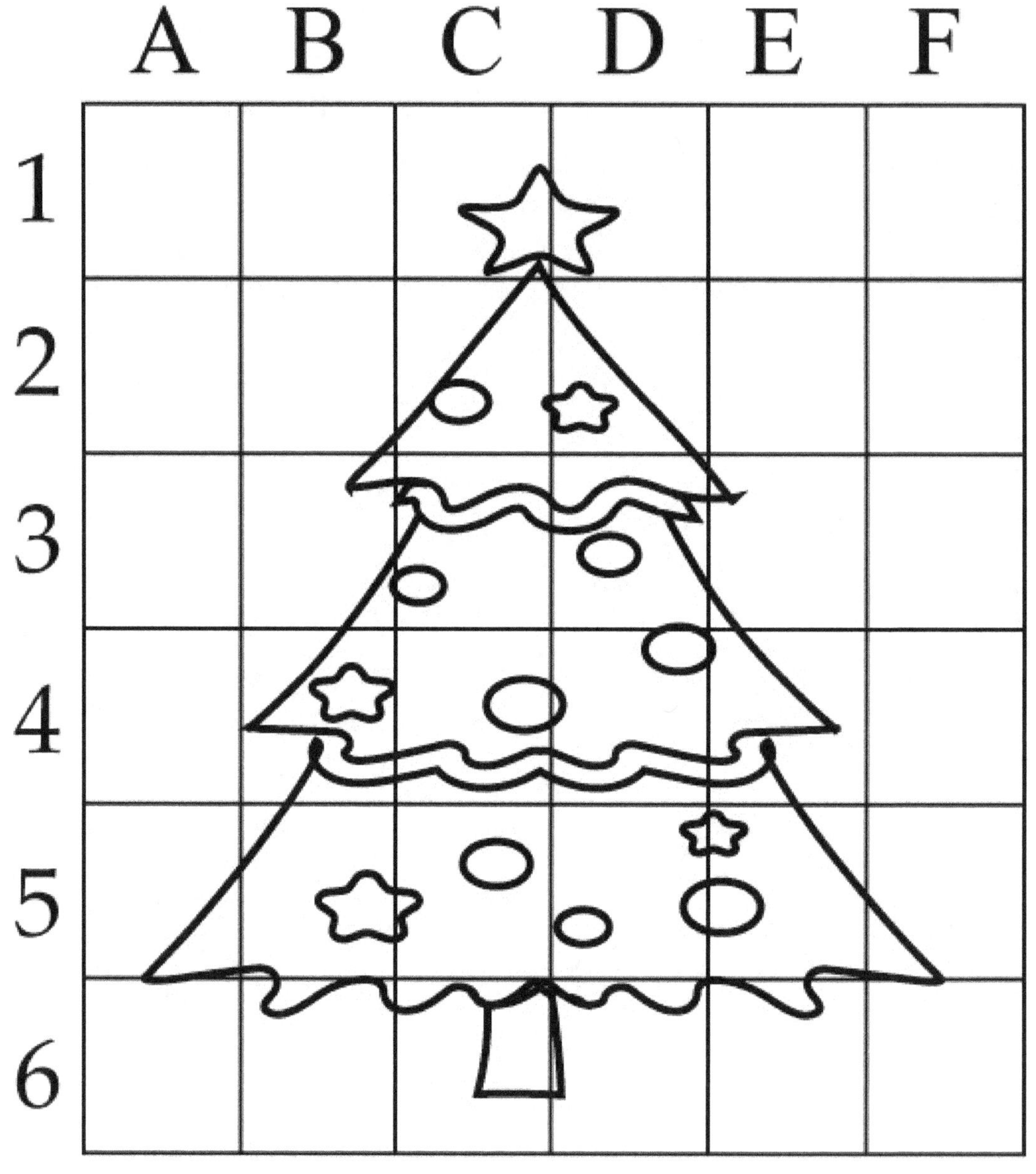

Now you do it!

	A	B	C	D	E	F
1						
2						
3						
4						
5						
6						

Try to trace it!

Draw it here!

Let's draw a guitar

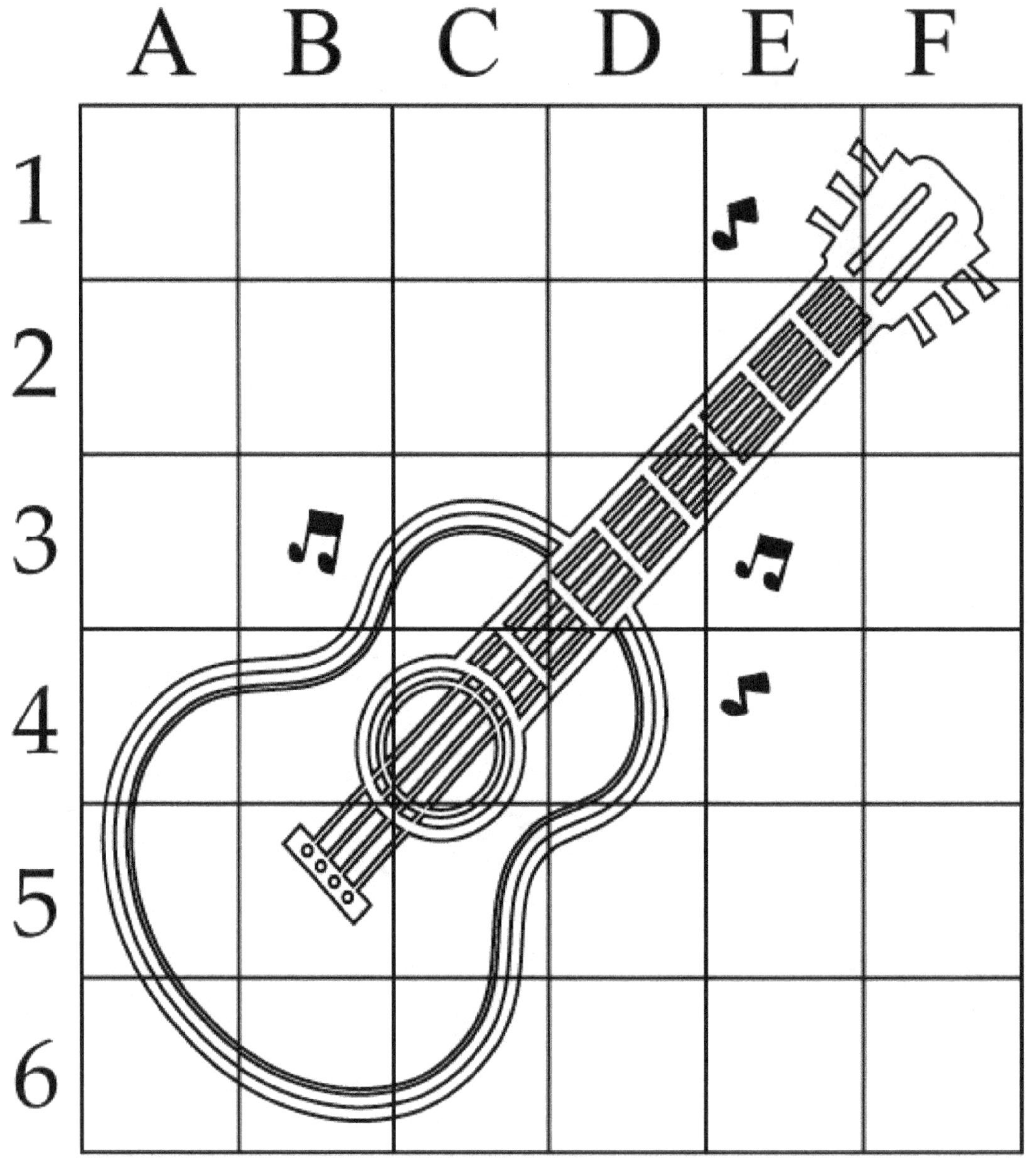

Now you do it!

	A	B	C	D	E	F
1						
2						
3						
4						
5						
6						

Try to trace it!

Draw it here!

Let's draw a saxophone

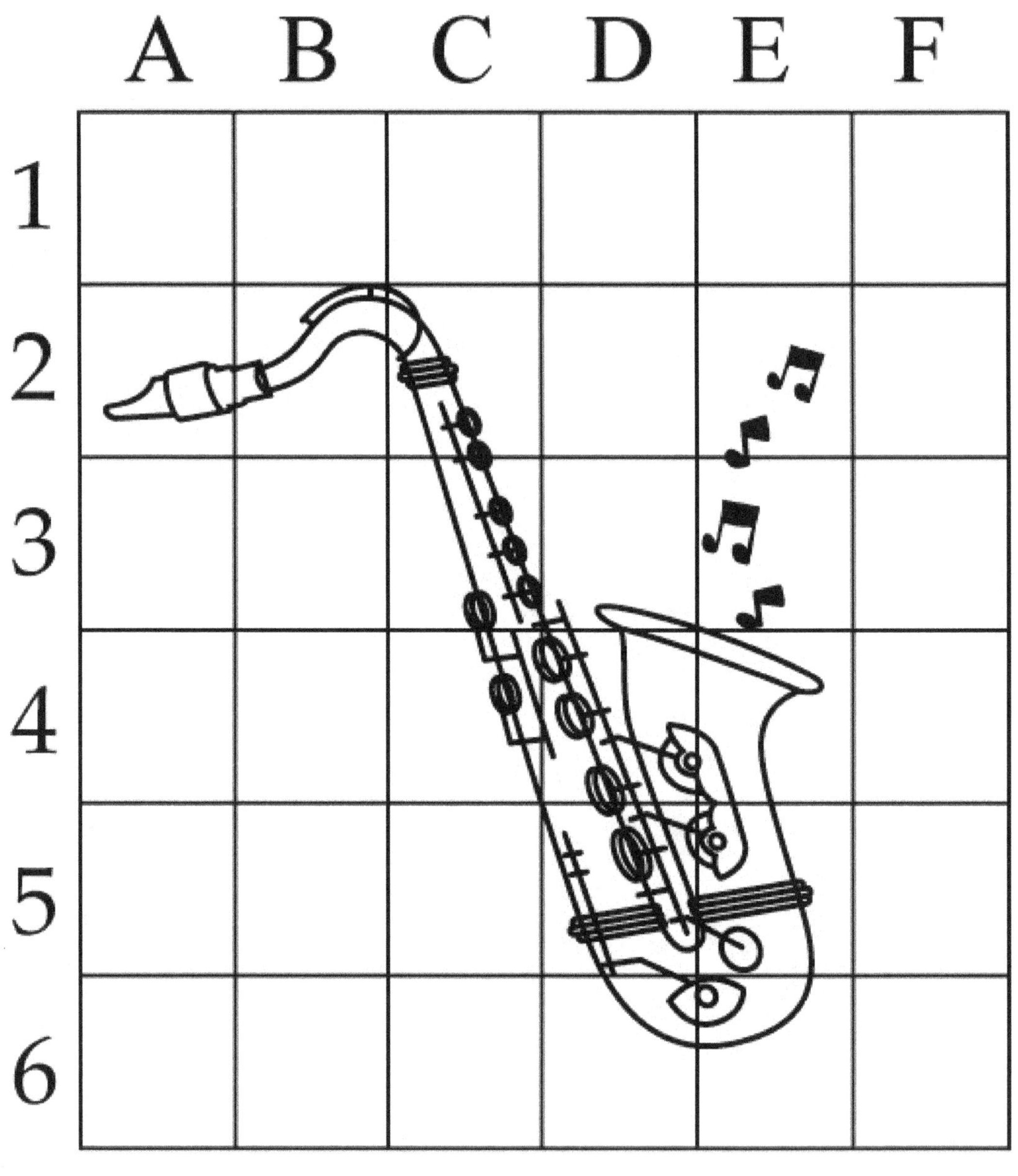

Now you do it!

	A	B	C	D	E	F
1						
2						
3						
4						
5						
6						

Try to trace it!

Draw it here!

Let's draw a cello

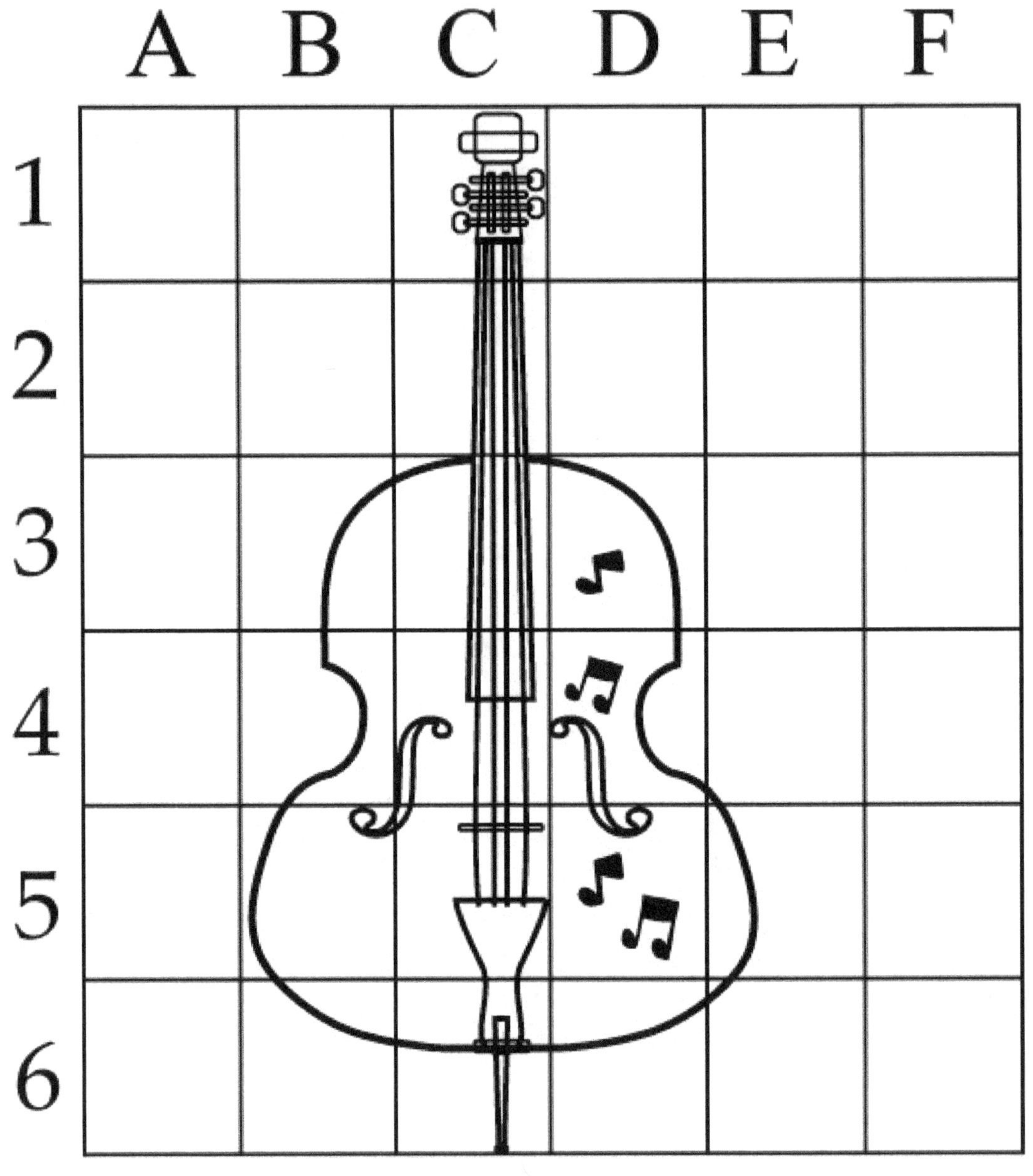

Now you do it!

	A	B	C	D	E	F
1						
2						
3						
4						
5						
6						

Try to trace it!

Draw it here!